聽說讀打寫

Textbook
(Traditional Character Edition)

IQChinese 策畫主編
Developed by IQChinese

Andover • Melbourne • Mexico City • Stamford, CT • Toronto • Hong Kong • New Delhi • Seoul • Singapore • Tokyo

Go! Chinese Go700 Textbook
(Traditional Character Edition)

Developed by IQChinese

Publishing Director:
Roy Lee

Editorial Manager, CLT:
Lan Zhao

Development Editor:
Coco Koh

Associate Development Editor:
Titus Teo

Senior Product Manager (Asia):
Joyce Tan

Product Manager (Outside Asia):
Mei Yun Loh

Creative Manager:
Melvin Chong

Regional Manager, Production & Rights:
Pauline Lim

Senior Production Executive:
Cindy Chai

Production Executive:
Evan Wu

Freelance Designer:
Jane Goh

© 2014 Cengage Learning Asia Pte Ltd

ALL RIGHTS RESERVED. No part of this work covered by the copyright herein may be reproduced, transmitted, stored or used in any form or by any means graphic, electronic, or mechanical, including but not limited to photocopying, recording, scanning, digitalizing, taping, Web distribution, information networks, or information storage and retrieval systems, without the prior written permission of the publisher.

For product information and technology assistance, contact us at
Cengage Learning Asia Customer Support, 65-6410-1200

For permission to use material from this text or product,
submit all requests online at **www.cengageasia.com/permissions**
Further permission questions can be emailed to
asia.permissionrequest@cengage.com

ISBN-13: 978-981-4455-25-1
ISBN-10: 981-4455-25-3

Cengage Learning Asia Pte Ltd
151 Lorong Chuan
#02-08 New Tech Park
Singapore 556741

Cengage Learning is a leading provider of customized learning solutions with office locations around the globe, including Andover, Melbourne, Mexico City, Stamford (CT), Toronto, Hong Kong, New Delhi, Seoul, Singapore, and Tokyo. Locate your local office at **www.cengage.com/global**

Cengage Learning products are represented in Canada by Nelson Education, Ltd.

For product information, visit **www.cengageasia.com**

Photo credits:
Thinkstock, Getty Images

Printed in Taiwan
2 3 4 5 17 16 15 14 13

Acknowledgements

Go! Chinese is designed to be used together with **IQChinese Go** courseware, a series of multimedia CD-ROMs developed by **IQChinese**.

This series of textbooks, workbooks, and CD-ROMs would not have been possible without the contribution of the following experienced and dedicated individuals:

- **Chia-Wei Lee** (Instruction Specialist, IQChinese)
- **Mei-Hui Lee** (for contributing to the content of the CD-ROMs)
- **Hsiang-Yun Liang** (for contributing to the content of the CD-ROMs)
- **Julie Lo** (for advising on the pedagogy and curriculum)
- **Yi-Hua Tseng** (for contributing to the content of the books)
- **I-Min Huang** (for contributing to the content of the books)
- **Hui-Chuan Wang** (for contributing to the content of the books and CD-ROMs)
- **Lanni Wang** (Instruction Specialist, IQChinese)
- **Meng-Tien Wu** (Instruction Manager, IQChinese)
- **Emily Yih** (for designing and planning the curriculum)
- **Ying-Xue Zhao** (for writing the reading texts which are age-appropriate and interesting)

We would also like to thank the following individuals who offered many helpful insights, ideas, and suggestions for improvement during the product development stage of **Go! Chinese**.

- **Jessie Lin Brown**, Singapore American School, Singapore
- **Deborah Chen**, Shammah Chinese School, USA
- **Henny Chen**, Moreau Catholic High School, USA
- **Yeafen Chen**, University of Wisconsin-Milwaukee, USA
- **Ting Ting Huang**, Grace Christian College, Philippines
- **Yi Liang Jiang**, Beijing Language and Culture University, China
- **Yan Jin**, Singapore American School, Singapore
- **Kerman Kwan**, Irvine Chinese School, USA
- **Andrew Scrimgeour**, University of South Australia, Australia
- **James L. Tan**, Grace Christian College, Philippines
- **Man Tao**, Koning Williem I College, the Netherlands
- **Chiungwen Tsai**, Westside Chinese School, USA
- **Tina Wu**, Westside High School, USA
- **YaWen (Alison) Yang**, Concordian international School, Thailand

Preface

Go! Chinese, together with ***IQChinese Go* multimedia CD-ROM**, is a fully-integrated Chinese language program that offers an easy, enjoyable, and effective learning experience for learners of Chinese as a foreign language.

The themes and lesson plans of this program are designed with references to the American National Standards for Foreign Language Learning developed by ACTFL[1], and the Curriculum Guides for Modern Languages developed by the Toronto District Board of Education. The program aims to help learners develop their communicative competence in the four language skills of listening, speaking, reading, and writing while gaining an appreciation of the Chinese culture. It allows learners to exercise their ability to compare and contrast different cultures, make connections with other discipline areas, and extend their learning experiences to their homes and communities.

The program employs innovative teaching methodologies and computer applications to enhance language learning, as well as keep students motivated in and outside of the classroom. The companion CD-ROM gives students access to audio, visual, and textual information about the language all at once. Chinese typing is systematically integrated into the program to facilitate the acquisition and retention of new vocabulary and to equip students with a skill that is becoming increasingly important in the Internet era wherein more and more professional and personal correspondence is done electronically.

Course Design

The program is divided into two series: Beginner and Intermediate. The Beginner Series, which comprises four levels (Go100-400), provides a solid foundation for continued study of the Intermediate Series (Go500-800). Each level includes a student text, a workbook, and a companion CD-ROM.

Beginner Series: Go100 – Go400

Designed for beginners, each level of the Beginner Series is made up of 10 colorfully illustrated lessons. Each lesson covers new vocabulary and simple sentence structures with particular emphasis on listening and speaking skills. In keeping with the communicative approach, a good mix of activities such as role play, interviews, games, pair work, and language exchanges are incorporated to allow students to learn to communicate through interaction in the target language. The CD-ROM uses rhythmic chants, word games, quizzes, and Chinese typing exercises to improve students' pronunciation, mastery of *pinyin*, and their ability to recognize and read words and sentences taught in each lesson.

The Beginner Series can be completed in roughly 240 hours (160 hours on Textbook and 80 hours on CD-ROM). Upon completion of the Beginner Series, the student will have acquired approximately 500 Chinese characters and 1000 common phrases.

Intermediate Series: Go500 – Go800

The Intermediate Series continues with the use of the communicative approach, but places a greater emphasis on Culture, Community, and Comparison. Through stories revolving around Chinese-American families, students learn vocabulary necessary for expressing themselves in a variety of contexts, describing their world, and discussing cultural differences.

The Intermediate Series can be completed in roughly 320 hours (240 hours on Textbook and 80 hours on CD-ROM). Upon completion of both the Beginner and Intermediate Series, the student will have acquired approximately 1000 Chinese characters and 2400 common phrases.

---

[1] American Council on the Teaching of Foreign Languages (http://www.actfl.org)

Course Features

Vocabulary and Sentence Structures

The program places emphasis on helping students use the target language in contexts relevant to their everyday lives. Therefore, the chosen vocabulary and sentence structures are based on familiar topics such as family, school activities, hobbies, weather, shopping, food, pets, modes of transport, etc. The same topics are revisited throughout the series to reinforce learning, as well as to expand on the vocabulary and sentence structures acquired before.

Listening and Speaking

Communicative activities encourage and require a learner to speak with and listen to other learners. Well-designed and well-executed communicative activities can help turn the language classroom into an active and enjoyable place where learners are motivated to learn and can learn what they need. The program integrates a variety of communicative activities such as role play, interviews, games, pair work, and language exchanges to give students the opportunity to put what they have learned into practice.

Word Recognition and Reading

Each lesson introduces about 12 new Chinese characters. Using the spiral approach, each new character is first introduced and then repeated in classroom activities and subsequent lessons to enhance the retention of new vocabulary over time. From level Go500, instead of chants, students are exposed to passages which are approximately 500 words long. Through these reading passages, students are continually exposed to vocabulary, both old and new, and this also hones their reading skills. Exercises after the passages encourage critical thinking and discussion, stretching the students' comprehension skills and their capability to express themselves.

Pinyin (phonetic notation) is added above newly introduced characters so that students can learn to pronounce them. To make sure students do not become over-reliant on *pinyin* to read Chinese, recycled vocabulary is stripped of *pinyin* so that students can learn to recognize and read the actual written characters in due course. For the same reason, the CD-ROM companion does not display the *pinyin* of words automatically.

Culture

Cultural content is assimilated into each of the topics to allow students to get to know about different cultures. This also allows them to identify themselves in relation to the cultures introduced. Each volume also includes general knowledge components on the Chinese language to develop the students' understanding and appreciation of the language.

Type-to-Learn Methodology

The unique characteristic of this series is the use of Chinese typing as an instructional strategy to improve listening, pronunciation, and word recognition. Activities in the CD-ROM require students to type characters or sentences as they are read aloud or displayed on the computer screen. Students will be alerted if they make a mistake and will be given the chance to correct them. If they do not get it right on the third try, the software provides immediate feedback on how to correct the error. This interactive trial-and-error process allows students to develop self-confidence and learn the language by doing.

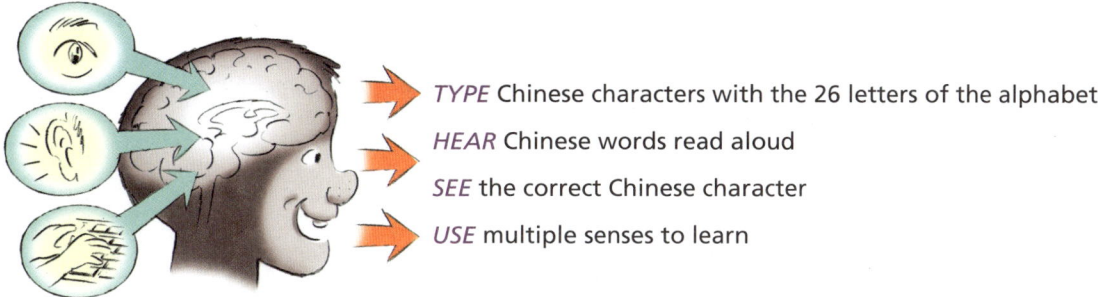

TYPE Chinese characters with the 26 letters of the alphabet

HEAR Chinese words read aloud

SEE the correct Chinese character

USE multiple senses to learn

Preface

Chinese Characters and Character Writing

The program does not require the student to be able to write all the core vocabulary; the teacher may however assign more character writing practice according to his or her classroom emphasis and needs. What the program aims to do is to give students a good grasp of Chinese radicals and stroke order rules, as well as to help students understand and appreciate the characteristics and formation of Chinese characters. The program includes writing practice on frequently used characters. Understanding the semantic function radicals have in the characters they form and having the ability to see compound characters by their simpler constituents enable students to memorize new characters in a logical way.

Using the CD-ROM as an Instructional Aid

The following diagram shows how a teacher might use the CD-ROM as an instructional aid to improve traditional classroom instruction.

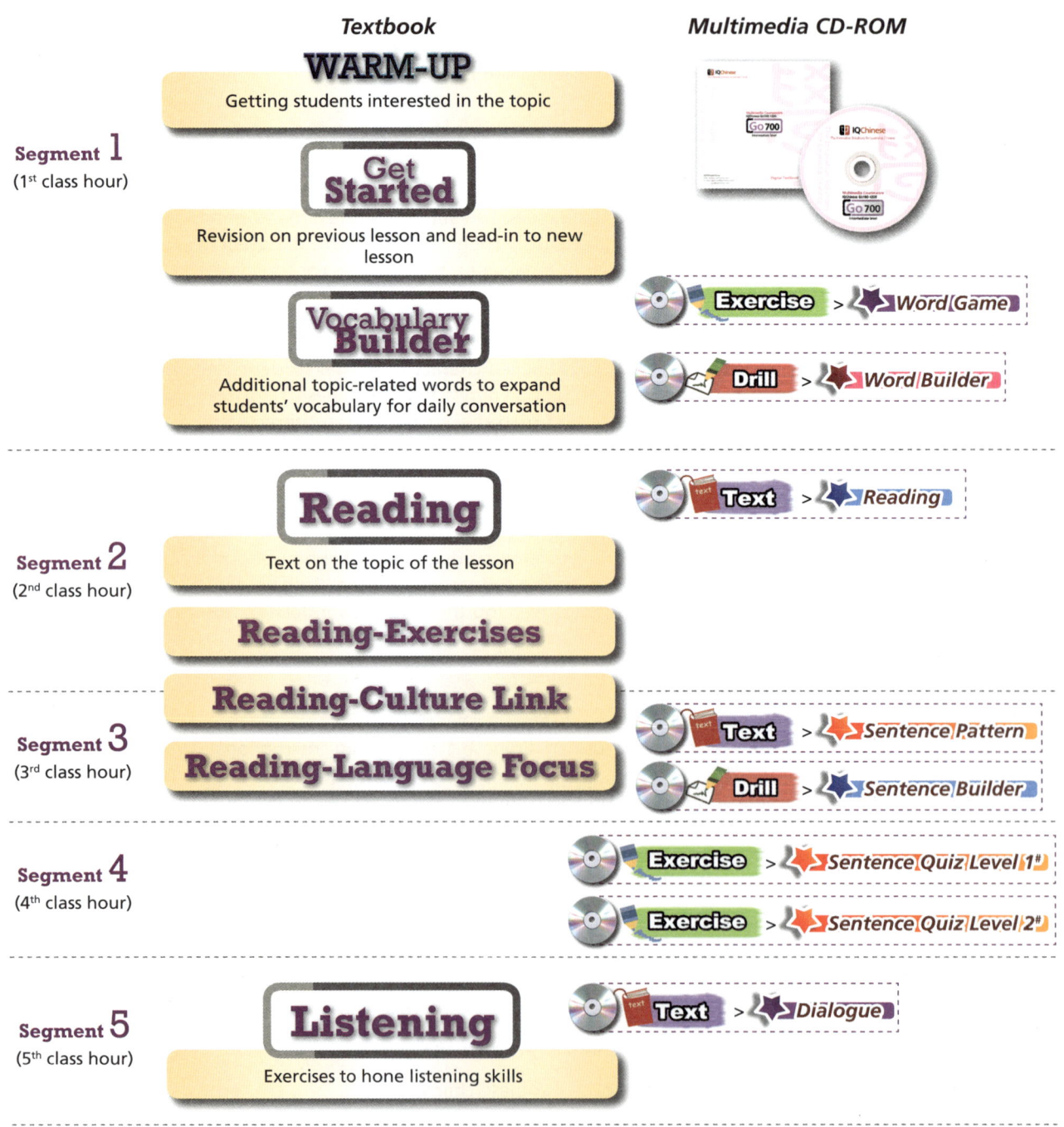

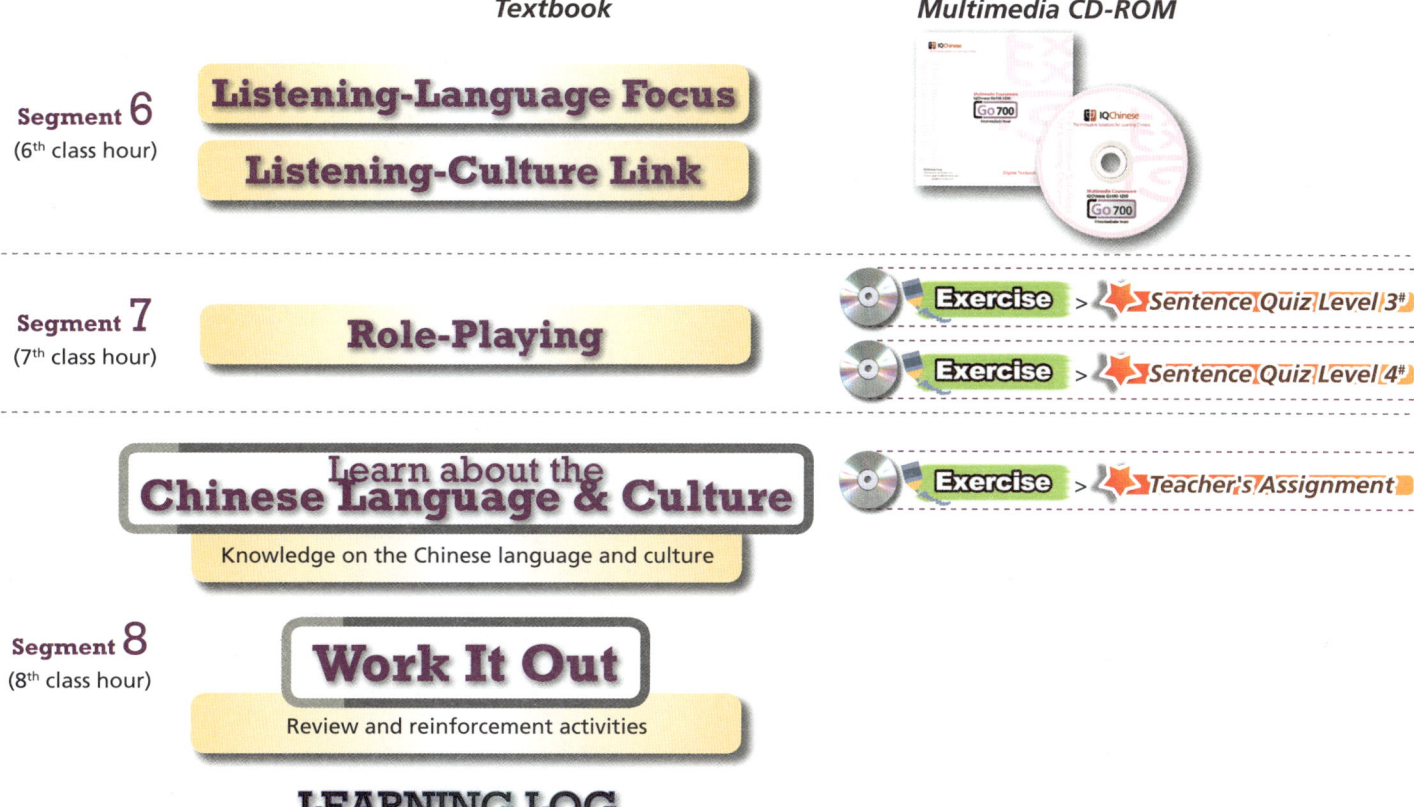

The section *Exercise > Sentence Quiz* on the CD-ROM enhances learning by stimulating multiple senses as well as providing immediate feedback on students' performance.

The Sentence Quiz exercise comprises four levels.

- Level 1 – Warm-up Quiz (Look, Listen, and Type): Chinese text, *pinyin*, and audio prompts are provided.
- Level 2 – Audio-aid Quiz: Only audio prompts are provided.
- Level 3 – Sentence Quiz: Reorder the words to form proper sentences.
- Level 4 – Comprehension Quiz: Type in the correct answers according to the content of the Reading and Dialogue components.

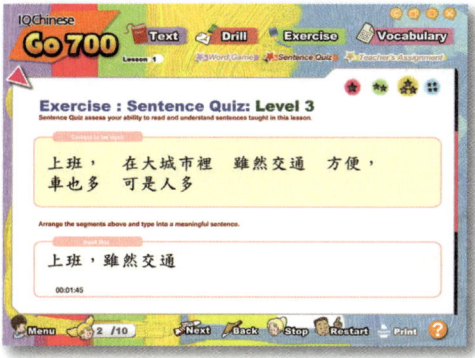

Type in the correct answer in the correct sequence, or according to the content of the text. This exercise tests the students' understanding of sentence patterns and comprehension skills.

Preface

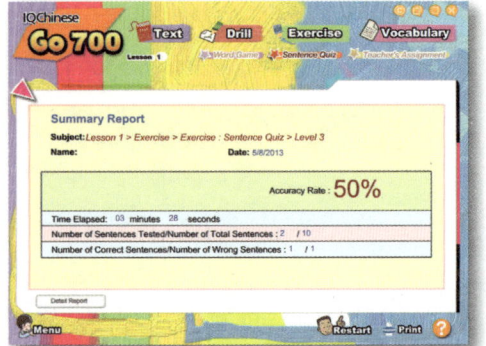

Summary report provides the percentage of correct answers given by the student, the total number of questions tried, and the total time spent on the exercise.

Detail report provides the correct answer to each question and a record of the student's answers.

Classroom Setup and Equipment

For small classes (up to 5 students), the teacher can show the CD-ROM features on one computer with students gathered around the screen. For large groups, a projector will be needed to project the computer's display onto a large screen so that the entire class can see.

If the classroom is not equipped with computers, the teacher may have students bring their own portable computers to class so that they can work individually or in small groups of 2 to 3 on the CD-ROM activities during designated class hours. CD-ROM activities may also be assigned as homework.

Suggestions for Teachers

We recommend that the teacher

- spend 6-7 hours on each lesson in the Textbook and 2 hours on each lesson on the CD-ROM. The course materials and lesson length may be adjusted according to students' proficiency level and learning ability.
- Adopt the lesson plans based on students' language ability and classroom learning hours. The basic course (marked as ☆ in the lesson plans) builds a solid fondation in mastering the Chinese language; while the advanced course (marked as ☆☆ in the lesson plans) allow students to have additional practice using the multimedia CD-ROM.
- allocate 1-2 class hours to go over with the students the Review units in the Workbook as a way to check on their progress.
- have the students complete 1-2 pages of the Workbook after every two class sessions.
- encourage the students to spend 10 minutes a day on the Sentence Quiz in the CD-ROM. Practice makes perfect!

More Support

IQChinese is the publisher for *IQChinese Go* multimedia CD-ROMs. By adopting Type-To-Learn as its core methodology, IQChinese provides learners of the Chinese language a complete solution to learn the language effectively.

Courseware & Homework

IQChinese offers additional resources for both teachers and students:

eClass (http://eclass.iqchinese.com): offers additional lesson-by-lesson practices, and allows teachers to create own assignments and quizzes.

IQChinese Fun (http://www.iqchinesefun.com): visit the website or use mobile applications for iPhone, iPad, and iPod Touch to learn and practice Chinese characters in a fun and interesting way.

- "Type-to-Learn" courseware for PC & Mac
- textbook & workbook
- online practice system
- mobile practice apps for iOS
- Chinese learning software

Teaching Support

Online teacher workshops, additional classroom activities and resources such as detailed chapter-by-chapter lesson plans, teaching slides, and supplementary assignments are developed to facilitate classroom teaching. Visit the following websites for more information.

Cengage Learning — http://www.cengageasia.com

IQChinese Teacher's Club — http://www.iqchinese.com

- online teaching resources
- teacher training & workshops
- supporting software

Technical Support

IQChinese offers technical support for product installation, school site licensing, digital lesson planning, etc. If you require technical assistance, please contact iqservice@iqchinese.com .

- product installation
- school site license
- digital learning conversion
- digital teaching planning

Preface ix

Scope & Sequence

Words marked with an asterisk (*) are supplementary vocabulary.

Lesson	Communicative Goals	Vocabulary	Language Focus	Cultural & Language Knowledge
小城故事 The Story of a Small Town **1**	• Describe the differences between a big city and a small town • Provide additional details on a subject • Describe the distance between two places • List items of a similar nature to elaborate on a topic	Characteristics of big cities and small towns 表演, 欣賞, 音樂會, 大自然, 國家公園, 操場, 鄉下, 海邊, 便利, 享受, 美食, 成長, 各國, 舉辦, 食物, 游泳, 功夫, 零用錢, 北歐, 觀光客, 風景, 商場 *戲劇, 舞蹈, 藝術, 樂團, 博物館, 美術館, 教堂, 展覽館, 休閒娛樂, 放鬆, 慢跑, 海景, 海風, 觀光, 景點, 紀念品, 名產, 明信片	• "不但……，還……" 住在小城裡，不但可以享受大城市的方便，還可以欣賞小城市的可愛。 • "……離……" 小城離海邊很近。 • "……，像……什麼的" 這裡的商店也賣各國的東西，像各國的食物，北歐的桌椅，南美洲的衣服什麼的。	• Chinatown • Sequence of the Chinese characters that made up of a word
歷史考試 The History Test **2**	• Describe my learning experience • Illustrate the main point or technique required to carry out a specified action • Describe the situation of failing to achieve the target despite having put in one's best • Express that an outcome remains unchanged even if a hypothetical situation or condition is present	Exams and subjects 傳記, 年代, 事件, 準備, 退步, 好夢, 遍, 原因, 結果, 看法, 弄懂, 記性, 想法, 即使, 晚安, 難怪 *代表, 科目, 化學, 自然科學, 生物, 物理, 外語, 複習, 口試, 筆試, 實驗, 分數, 粗心, 細心, 惡夢, 睡過頭, 熬夜, 遲到	• "……，最重要的是，……" 讀歷史，最重要的是，要知道事件發生的原因和結果。 • "……，……怎麼……都……" 有些名字和年代，我怎麼背都背不下來。 • "即使……，也……" 即使都記住了，也很快就忘了。	• Exam culture in Asia • Exam-related Chinese idioms
校外教學 A Field Trip **3**	• State the preparation to make and things to note with regard to a school field trip • Describe doing things in sequence • Repeatedly remind and urge a person to do something • Refute a certain viewpoint or give opposing views	Preparation of a school field trip 紀念品, 濕/濕濕的, 防滑, 雨衣, 晒傷, 防晒, 防晒油, 興奮, 校外教學, 船, 糖果, 防水, 講課, 千萬, 掉, 海洋, 生物, 筆記, 麻煩, 漁夫, 救生衣, 趕快, 當心 *紀念日, 紀念碑, 紀念館, 乾/乾乾的, 雨鞋, 太陽眼鏡, 戶外, 蚊蟲, 野餐, 郊遊, 失望, 期待	• "一 + Measure Word + 一 + Measure Word (地) + Verb Phrase" 把下星期要帶的東西一樣一樣(地)寫出來。 • "千萬……" 千萬別掉到海裡去了。 • "……才……" 你才是大胖子呢！	• One of the great inventions of ancient China – compass • Formation of Chinese words

Lesson	Communicative Goals	Vocabulary	Language Focus	Cultural & Language Knowledge
退休生活 Life after Retirement **4**	• Tell the similarities and differences between Eastern and Western perspectives on retirement • Express opinions from someone else's perspective • State a hypothetical situation and ask for other people's opinion • Provide options in a question • Make a conclusion based on what has been said	Retirement 退休, 故鄉, 爬山, 熟悉, 獨立, 年紀, 平常, 互相, 老人, 差, 比較, 忍受, 飛盤 *退休金, 養老院, 獨自, 孤單, 單獨, 陪伴, 忍耐, 忍心, 忍讓, 忍不住, 農村, 森林, 湖畔, 陌生, 依賴, 自由, 拘束, 接近, 遠離	• "對……來說，……" 很冷，很熱，對外公外婆來說，都是可以忍受的。 • "要是……，怎麼辦？" 要是你們跟朋友都搬到很遠的地方去, (我)怎麼辦？ • "……是……，還是……？" 我是留在這裡，還是搬到別的地方去？ • "這麼說，……" 這麼說，要是你們搬到很遠的地方，我也可以坐飛機去看你們！	• Different views between the East and the West on retirement and living with extended families • Form of Chinese seven-character-quatrain poems (七言絕句) • Chinese poem "回鄉偶書" (Returning to My Hometown)
熱鬧的選舉 The Exciting Election **5**	• State the prerequisites of an election candidate and different electoral campaigns • Describe how an item is used at a certain location to complete an action • Express the conditions to be fulfilled before a target can be achieved	Election and electoral campaigns 選舉, 競選, 投/投票, 候選人, 當選, 負責, 幫助, 熱鬧, 簡單, 海報, 學生會, 管, 會長, 進行, 上台, 演講, 心思, 畫, 演, 短劇, 相信, 能力, 本來 *落選, 助選員, 政見, 協助, 支持, 冷清, 複雜, 公正, 偏私, 圖畫, 圖案, 賄賂, 利益, 不擇手段, 秉公無私	• "……用……在……" 以思用很多張玩具錢，在海報上排出了自己的名字。 • "只有……，才……" 只有大家都相信、都喜歡的人才會被選上。	• Election culture in different countries • Usage of Chinese antithesis (對偶)
旅行學習 Traveling and Learning **6**	• Describe the relationship between traveling and learning • Narrate personal traveling experience in full • Express an action and the duration of the action • Describe how certain conditions have to be fulfilled before a target can be met	Traveling and preparation work 查, 安排, 旅行箱, 上網, 開會, 東方, 出發, 會話, 印, 列, 聯絡, 另外, 花, 地點, 知識, 大廈, 古老 *預訂, 機票, 旅館, 簽證, 護照, 保險, 駕照, 行李, 資料, 行程, 住宿, 外幣, 登記, 機位, 準時, 提前, 延後, 誤點	• " Verb (了) + Time + Noun" 開 (了) 三天的會。 • "……需要……，才……" 他們需要做好出發前的準備，才會有快樂的旅行。	• Travel taboos in different countries • Evolution of Chinese scripts/calligraphy
爸爸失業了 Dad Is Out of Work **7**	• State the importance of increasing income and reducing expenditure • Describe the methods required to resolve a certain problem • Express that one does not have an opinion, interest, or notion regarding a particular subject	Facing difficult times together with the family and solutions to deal with the difficulties 減少, 公司, 情形, 花費, 繼續, 人員, 失業, 政府, 失業金, 打算, 抱住 *開除, 裁員, 職業, 正職, 兼職, 存錢, 薪水, 時薪, 月薪, 年薪, 學費, 增加, 節省, 浪費, 支出, 收入, 節儉, 奢侈, 開源節流, 克勤克儉, 揮金如土	• "……，得……" 你們公司不太賺錢，得減少花費。 • "……對……一點兒……都沒有" 我對電腦一點兒興趣都沒有。	• Wage system in different countries • Chinese metaphors (比喻詞)

Scope & Sequence

Lesson	Communicative Goals	Vocabulary	Language Focus	Cultural & Language Knowledge
精彩的奧運 The Exciting Olympics **8**	• State the meaning of sportsmanship and team spirit • Explain the cause and effect of a circumstance • Indicate a particular situation in which certain essential conditions must be fulfilled • Evaluate a topic stated earlier	Olympics, sportsmanship, team spirit 奧運, 籃球, 體操, 跳水, 百米, 接力賽, 選手, 加油, 運動精神, 公尺, 接, 棒子, 因此, 投/投籃, 隊長, 球員, 得分, 配合, 對手, 看(kān), 團隊, 動作, 秒, 隊友, 尖叫, 表現 *國家代表, 裁判, 犯規, 公平, 名次, 冠軍, 亞軍, 季軍, 獎盃, 獎牌, 破紀錄, 驕傲, 氣餒, 鼓勵	• "……，因此……" 接力賽不只要跑得快，接棒子的時候還要接得好，因此選手們還是需要練習很多次。 • "……一定要……才行" 打籃球的時候，所有的球員一定要一起合作才行。 • "……Verb + 起來……" 哥哥今天的表現，聽起來真是精彩極了！	• Origins of the Olympic Games • Concept of the the Chinese saying "勝不驕, 敗不餒" • Alternative usage of the the Chinese negation word 不
孔子 Confucius **9**	• State who Confucius is and his school of thought • Express the key point in one's opinion • Use an emphatic tone to express an uncommon situation	Confucius, respect for teachers 偉大, 偉人, 必, 仁愛, 禮/禮節, 尊敬, 下棋, 孔子, 道理, 認為, 行禮, 習慣, 地位, 節, 銅像 *雄偉, 不必, 必要, 必須, 禮儀, 尊重, 重視, 跳棋, 象棋, 圍棋, 騎馬, 射箭, 君子, 小人, 至聖先師, 尊師重道	• "……認為……最重要" 孔子認為「仁愛」和「禮節」最重要。 • "連……都……" 連日本人都知道孔子。	• Confucianism • Famous quotes from the *Analects of Confucius* (《論語》) • Different views between the East and the West on the role of teachers
端午節 The Dragon Boat Festival **10**	• Describe customs and activities of the Dragon Boat Festival • Express the targets met or actions taken after certain conditions are fulfilled • Explain the objective of a topic • State a situation in which there are no exceptions	Dragon Boat Festival and its customs 划船, 龍舟賽, 打鼓, 旗子, 粽子, 國王, 市長, 人民, 河, 水上運動, 報名, 划, 龍船, 影片, 端午節, 詩人, 辦法, 包, 口味, 鹹, 肉 *鼓手, 香包, 艾草, 習俗, 國旗, 畫龍點睛, 栩栩如生, 河流, 衝浪, 潛水	• "(Question Word)……就……" 哪一隊先拿到旗子就贏。 • "……是為了……" 端午節是為了紀念一位中國詩人。 • "什麼……都……" 什麼事情都需要練習。	• Qu Yuan (屈原), the patriotic poet • Customs of the Dragon Boat Festival • A Chinese poem about the Dragon Boat Festival

Table of Contents

ACKNOWLEDGEMENTS iii

PREFACE iv

SCOPE & SEQUENCE x

LESSON 1 小城故事 The Story of a Small Town ... 1

LESSON 2 歷史考試 The History Test ... 15

LESSON 3 校外教學 A Field Trip ... 29

LESSON 4 退休生活 Life after Retirement ... 43

LESSON 5 熱鬧的選舉 The Exciting Election ... 59

LESSON 6 旅行學習 Traveling and Learning ... 73

LESSON 7 爸爸失業了 Dad Is Out of Work ... 87

LESSON 8 精彩的奧運 The Exciting Olympics ... 101

LESSON 9 孔子 Confucius ... 115

LESSON 10 端午節 The Dragon Boat Festival ... 129

VOCABULARY INDEX ... 145

FORMS: Lesson 1 Survey Form ... 157

Lesson 2 Survey Form ... 159

Lesson 6 Holiday Planning Form ... 161

LESSON 1

小城故事
The Story of a Small Town

1. Where are these places?
2. Which of these places do you prefer to live in?

My Goals

1. Describe the differences between a big city and a small town
2. Provide additional details on a subject
3. Describe the distance between two places
4. List items of a similar nature to elaborate on a topic
5. Understand that the meaning of a Chinese word may change when the order of the characters that made up the word changes
6. Appreciate the phenomenon that Chinese people in a foreign land seek to retain their culture

Get Started

A Number the following text in the correct order to form a coherent conversation.

SCENARIO: After school, 以晴 and 久美子 are discussing where to go this weekend.

[2] 以　晴：可是到大城市去玩，要坐一個多小時的車，還要花很多錢。還是留在小城吧！

[7] 久美子：當然想！妳說得對，只要跟好朋友一起，不管去哪裡，都很有意思。

[4] 以　晴：這個週末不一樣，小城有慶祝活動，很有趣的。

[1] 久美子：週末我們去大城市玩，好不好？

[5] 久美子：不管多麼有趣，那麼小的地方，我一下子就走完了，一點意思也沒有。

[3] 久美子：我住在這裡這麼久了，小城什麼地方，我都去過了。

[6] 以　晴：有沒有意思都是看妳跟誰一起玩來決定的。妳不想跟我一起參加慶祝活動嗎？

[8] 以　晴：那麼，就這麼說定了，這個週末我們在小城玩吧！

B In pairs, practice reading out the above conversation. Next, exchange roles and repeat the exercise.

LESSON 1

| biǎo yǎn 表演 | xīn shǎng 欣賞 | yīn yuè huì 音樂會 | | bó wù guǎn 博物館 (museum) | měi shù guǎn 美術館 (art gallery) |

| xì jù 戲劇 (theatrical plays) | wǔ dào 舞蹈 (dance) | yì shù 藝術 (arts) | yuè tuán 樂團 (orchestra) | jiào táng 教堂 (church) | zhǎn lǎn guǎn 展覽館 (exhibition center) |

| dà zì rán 大自然 | guó jiā gōng yuán 國家公園 | cāo chǎng 操場 | | xiāng xià 鄉下 | hǎi biān 海邊 |

| xiū xián yú lè 休閒娛樂 (leisure and recreation) | fàng sōng 放鬆 (relax) | màn pǎo 慢跑 (jog) | | hǎi jǐng 海景 (sea view) | hǎi fēng 海風 (sea breeze) |

| guān guāng 觀光 (sightseeing) | jǐng diǎn 景點 (tourist attraction) | jì niàn pǐn 紀念品 (souvenir) | míng chǎn 名產 (local specialty) | míng xìn piàn 明信片 (postcard) |

New Words

biǎo yǎn 表演	performance	xīn shǎng 欣賞	appreciate	yīn yuè huì 音樂會	musical concert
dà zì rán 大自然	nature	guó jiā gōng yuán 國家公園	National Park	cāo chǎng 操場	sports ground
xiāng xià 鄉下	countryside	hǎi biān 海邊	seaside		

Memory Mix-and-Match

1. Divide the class into two groups. The teacher will prepare two sets of word cards and paste them facing inwards on the board.

2. While the teacher keeps track of time (50 seconds for each group), each group will take turns to send a representative to flip a card from each set. When two cards showing the same word are flipped, the student will have to read out the word. One score will be awarded for the correct answer.

3. The group with the highest score within the fixed time wins the game.

小城故事

Reading

SCENARIO: Living in a big city or a small town has its own advantages and disadvantages. Let's take a look at the neighborhood 以晴 lives in.

以晴的爸爸喜歡大自然，常常跟孩子們說他小時候住在鄉下的事。他希望以後能搬到國家公園附近，這樣就可以天天接近大自然。但是，以晴的媽媽不願意，因為她喜歡城市生活的便利，不但可以和好朋友一起欣賞音樂會，還可以享受美食；如果生病了，去醫院看病也方便。

以晴的爸爸在大城市裡上班，雖然交通方便，可是人多車也多，他不太喜歡，所以在大城市附近的小城買了房子。以晴的爸爸說，讓孩子在小城裡上學、成長，❶不但可以享受大城市的方便，還可以欣賞小城市的可愛。只是，他每天要早起，開一個多小時的車去上班。

小城裡住了來自世界各國的人。以晴算過，除了英文，全校學生會說的語言一共有三十一種。所以，每次小城舉辦美食節，都看得到各國精彩的表演，吃得到各國的美食，還能學到一些各國食物的名字。

❷ 小城離海邊很近，夏天媽媽常常帶以晴他們去游泳、跑步，也常有很多不同國家的人在海邊唱歌、跳舞；他們會用自己的語言向大家問好。以思說他可以在海邊表演中國功夫、唱中文歌，一邊練習中文，一邊賺零用錢。

因為小城裡住了很多不同國家的人，所以這裡的商店也賣各國的東西，❸ 像各國的食物、北歐的桌椅、南美洲的衣服什麼的。到了週末和暑假，還有很多人到小城來玩。那時候，爸爸就會說，今天我們留在家裡好了，把美麗的小城讓給觀光客吧！

New Words

便利 biàn lì — convenient	享受 xiǎng shòu — enjoy	美食 měi shí — delicacies	成長 chéng zhǎng — grow up
各國 gè guó — various countries	舉辦 jǔ bàn — hold (an event)	食物 shí wù — food	游泳 yóu yǒng — swimming
功夫 gōng fū — kung fu; martial arts	零用錢 líng yòng qián — pocket money	北歐 běi ōu — Northern Europe	觀光客 guān guāng kè — tourists

Exercises

Check the Answers

Check the correct descriptions of the neighborhood that 以晴 and her family live in.

- ☐ 1. 生活便利的大城市 (biàn lì)
- ☑ 2. 在大城市附近的小城
- ☐ 3. 上學要坐一個小時的車
- ☑ 4. 有很多從不同國家來的人
- ☐ 5. 學生要學三十一種語言
- ☑ 6. 週末會舉辦美食節 (jǔ bàn měi shí)
- ☑ 7. 去游泳很方便 (yóu yǒng)
- ☐ 8. 適合冬天去玩
- ☑ 9. 有很多觀光客 (guān guāng kè)
- ☑ 10. 離海邊很近 (hǎi biān)
- ☐ 11. 在國家公園附近 (guó jiā gōng yuán)

Write an Introduction

Using the descriptions listed above, introduce the neighborhood that 以晴 and her family live in.

以晴住在一個大城市

Think & Discuss

Work in pairs and answer the questions in Chinese.

1. 小城和大城市有什麼不一樣的地方？
2. 以晴的爸爸和媽媽誰喜歡住在大城市，誰喜歡住在小城？為什麼？
3. 你喜歡住在大城市還是小城？為什麼？

小城故事

LESSON 1

Language Focus

1	住在小城裡，	不但	可以享受大城市的方便， xiǎng shòu
	明天學校有很多活動，		可以欣賞表演， xīn shǎng biǎo yǎn

還	可以欣賞小城市的可愛。 xīn shǎng
	可以參加音樂會。 yīn yuè huì

TIP: The paired conjunctions 不但 and 還 is used to provide additional details on the same subject. 不但 is used in the first clause after the subject while 還 leads the second clause to add more information.

A: 為什麼你喜歡去海邊？
　　　　　　　　　hǎi biān

B: 因為去海邊不但可以欣賞海景，還可以享受大自然。
　　　hǎi biān　　　　　xīn shǎng hǎi jǐng　　xiǎng shòu dà zì rán

A: 為什麼你喜歡過中秋節？

B: 因為中秋節時不但可以吃月餅，還能跟家人一起賞月。

Using sentence structure 1, complete the sentences with the helping phrases.

1. 我最喜歡那家餐廳，因為 __不但可以享受美食還可以欣賞音樂。__

2. 去博物館 __不但可以學習歷__

Group A	Group B
享受美食 xiǎng shòu měi shí	欣賞以前的人留下的東西 xīn shǎng
學習歷史	欣賞音樂 xīn shǎng

小城故事

2

小城	離	海邊 hǎi biān	很近。
哥哥的學校		國家公園 guó jiā gōng yuán	不遠。

nearest
not far

A: 快要上課了！
B: 操場(cāo chǎng)離教室有一點遠，我們走快一點兒吧！

A: 請問學校附近有美術館(měi shù guǎn)嗎？
B: 有，學校離美術館(měi shù guǎn)不太近，開車需要二十分鐘。

TIP The preposition 離 indicates distance between two fixed points. It introduces a point of reference (B) to the subject (A) in the pattern of "point A +離 + point B". An adjective phrase follows this pattern to describe the distance between points A and B. The distance can be expressed in a specific numerical term too.

PRACTICE IT Study the map carefully. Using sentence structure 2 and helping phrases, write sentences to express the distance between the places.

操場 cāo chǎng — 10 分鐘 — 博物館 bó wù guǎn — 5 分鐘 — 教堂 jiào táng

博物館 — 20 分鐘 — 國家公園 guó jiā gōng yuán

海邊 hǎi biān — 25 分鐘 — 國家公園

不近也不遠
很近
有一點遠
非常近

1. 博物館離教堂非常
2. 博
3.
4.

LESSON 1

3.
| 這裡的商店也賣各國的東西， | 像 | 各國的食物（gè guó shí wù）、 |
| 學校舉辦（jǔ bàn）很多課外活動， | | 唱歌比賽、 |

| 北歐（běi ōu）的桌椅、 | 南美洲的衣服 | 什麼的。 |
| 樂團表演（yuè tuán biǎo yǎn）、 | 電影欣賞（xīn shǎng） | |

A: 臺灣的年夜飯會吃什麼呢？
B: 臺灣的年夜飯會有很多菜，像魚、水餃、年糕什麼的。

A: 你喜歡什麼休閒（xiū xián）活動？
B: 我喜歡的休閒（xiū xián）活動很多，像游泳（yóu yǒng）、欣賞（xīn shǎng）戲劇（xì jù）、逛展覽（zhǎn lǎn）什麼的。

TIP: This sentence structure expresses items of a similar nature which are used for elaborating on a topic. The word 像 introduces a list of items associated with the topic stated before; the phrase 什麼的 indicates that there are other unmentioned items.

PRACTICE IT — Using sentence structure 3, complete the dialogues with the helping phrases.

1. A: 最近大城市會舉辦（jǔ bàn）哪些表演（biǎo yǎn）？
   B: 最近大城市 _會舉bàn很多biǎo演，xiāng 功夫。_

2. A: 旅行的時候你都會買什麼東西？
   B: 旅行的時候 _我_ _____

| jì niàn pǐn | yīn yuè huì | míng xìn piàn | míng chǎn | gōng fū | xì jù |
| 紀念品 | 音樂會 | 明信片 | 名產 | 功夫 | 戲劇 |

Check out the Text > Sentence Pattern section on the Go700 CD-ROM.

小城故事

Listening

Text > Dialogue section

SCENARIO: The weather today is good and Mother is bringing 以晴 and 以思 to the beach. They are talking about the advantages and disadvantages of living in a big city and a small town.

A Listen to the Go700 CD-ROM for the dialogue and answer the following multiple-choice questions.

1. 為什麼以晴覺得很舒服？
   (A) 因為可以在大城市看風景。
   (B) 因為可以在商場喝果汁。
   (C) 因為可以在海邊看風景。

2. 以思覺得住在小城怎麼樣？
   (A) 可以看風景，很舒服。
   (B) 買東西不方便。
   (C) 去海邊得坐一小時的車。

3. 以晴覺得住在大城市裡不能天天做什麼？
   (A) 坐車   (B) 看風景   (C) 買東西

4. 媽媽覺得住在哪裡比較好？
   (A) 大城市   (B) 小城   (C) 各有各的好

5. 下面哪一個句子是對的？
   (A) 以思和以晴最後都想住在大城市。
   (B) 媽媽覺得小城很可愛，但是不方便。
   (C) 不管大城市還是小城，喜歡自己住的地方最重要。

New Words

| fēng jǐng 風景 | scenery |
| shāng chǎng 商場 | shopping mall |

小城故事

LESSON 1

B Number the following text in the correct order to form a coherent conversation.

(6) 媽媽：以晴，妳喜歡住在小城裡，還是跟弟弟一樣，也想住在大城市裡？

(7) 以思：喜歡是喜歡，可是我們要到大城市去，dou de zuo 個多小 de _____，太麻煩了！

(4) 媽媽：大城市有大城市的_____，小城市有小城市的_____，最重要的是，我們要喜歡自己住的地方。不早了，我們應該回家了。

(1) 以晴：我最喜歡像這樣，坐在_____，真舒服！

(5) 媽媽：以思，你不喜歡我們住的小城嗎？

(3) 以思：可是，這裡沒有大商場(shāng chǎng)，買東西很不方便；_____，什麼都有，真方便！有時候我也想跟朋友到大商場(shāng chǎng)看看、買買東西。

(2) 以思：以晴說得對，住在大城市的人得_____才能看到美麗的風景(fēng jǐng)。我想，我還是住在小城裡好了。

(8) 以晴：我覺得雖然大城市裡有很多大商場(shāng chǎng)，可是我們不需要天天買東西。在這裡我們可以_____。

C Listen to the dialogue on the Go700 CD-ROM again, and fill in the blanks.

小城故事

Culture Link

Chinatown

When strangers meet in a foreign land, they often greet each other with a question "Where are you from?" Due to geographical reasons, people living in a particular region usually share similar accents, eating habits, as well as culture and customs. Hence, when people from the same locale meet in a foreign land, they develop a sense of closeness. In the early days when many Chinese people migrated overseas and became the minorities in their new country of residence, they tended to live near each other so as to face new challenges together. As time goes by, these communities eventually become the "Chinatown" that we know of today.

The Chinese names for "Chinatown" vary in different countries and places; the most common names are 唐人街 (tángrénjiē), 中國城 (zhōngguóchéng), 中華街 (zhōnghuájiē), and 華埠 (huábù).

 Is there a Chinatown in your city? Have you ever visited a Chinatown? If you did, what did you see there?

Form groups of five and role-play the scenario. You may use the sentence structures provided below.

CHARACTERS:

爸爸, 媽媽, 以安, 以晴, 以思

SCENARIO:
Yesterday was Saturday and Mother brought everyone to the city for a day trip. Today, in the living room, they are talking about the fun events that took place.

SENTENCE STRUCTURES:

1. 不但……，還……
2. ……離……
3. ……，像……什麼的
4. 如果……，就可以……
5. 除了……，還有……

LESSON 1

Learn about the Chinese Language & Culture

　　字和字加在一起成為詞，詞和詞放在一起成為句子。有些*語詞(yǔ cí)很有趣，前後交換了以後，有的意思還是一樣的，有的就變得不一樣了。

意思一樣的：

成長 / 長成	適合 / 合適	替代 / 代替
(grow up) (grow up)	(suitable) (suitable)	(substitute for) (substitute for)

意思不一樣的：

日本 / 本日	用功 / 功用	鄉下 / 下鄉
(Japan) (today)	(hardworking) (function)	(countryside) (going to the countryside)

兒女 / 女兒	願意 / 意願	山上 / 上山
(children) (daughter)	(willing) (wish; desire)	(on a hill) (go up a hill)

 Can you think of other similar words? Write them down below.

意思一樣的：媽媽,媽媽 / 爸爸,爸爸

意思不一樣的：山火,火山 / 文法,法文

*語詞 word and phrase

小城故事

Work It Out

Which cities have you been to? Among them, are there any cities that have left a lasting impression on you, and are there any cities that you do not wish to visit again?

TASK

Survey: Which is a better city to live in?

1. The teacher instructs students to cut out the survey form on page 157.
2. The class votes and chooses three different cities. For each of the cities, each student is to write down two reasons for liking it or for disliking it.
3. Interview at least three classmates. Write down the different views in the "Others" column. If the views are similar, the interviewee can sign next to the reasons in the "Myself" column.
4. Divide the class into groups to review and tabulate the most and least popular city to live in and the respective reasons.
5. Each group will collate and display the results in charts and present them in class.
6. After the presentation, each student is to fill in his/her favorite and least favorite city on the form.
7. The teacher may also keep track of the results on the board to tabulate the overall results for the class.

LEARNING LOG

I can...

	Excellent	Good	Fair	Need Improvement
1 state the differences between a big city and a small town.	○	○	○	○
2 use "不但……，還……" to provide additional details on a subject.	○	○	○	○
3 use "……離……" to describe the distance between two places.	○	○	○	○
4 use "……，像……什麼的" to list items of a similar nature to elaborate on a topic.	○	○	○	○
5 write 鄉下, 欣賞, 風景, and 享受.	○	○	○	○

小城故事

LESSON 2

歷史考試
The History Test

1. What is this student doing?
2. How do you prepare for your exam?

1. Describe my learning experience
2. Illustrate the main point or technique required to carry out a specific action
3. Describe the situation of failing to achieve the target despite having put in one's best
4. Express that an outcome remains unchanged even if a hypothetical situation or condition is present
5. Understand the exam culture in Asia as well as exam-related idioms and vocabulary

 **Get Started**

SCENARIO: 安地 and 阿明 visit 以晴 at her place. Her mother tells them that 以晴 is reading in her room.

A Fill in the blanks with the options provided below to complete the conversation.

安地：以晴，＿＿＿＿，妳怎麼現在就開始*複習了？

以晴：我想早一點開始看書，因為有一些學科，＿＿＿＿，前幾天才開始看，一定會看不完。

阿明：以晴說得對！安地，要考試了，你不緊張嗎？

安地：緊張是緊張，＿＿＿＿，我打算下個星期再開始看。

阿明：以晴，妳在看中文嗎？妳的中文學得這麼好，需要這麼早就開始複習嗎？

以晴：＿＿＿＿，考試前我都會複習很多次。

安地：聽妳這麼說，我也應該開始複習了。阿明，我們還是回家看書吧！

*複習 review

A. 不管學得好不好　　C. 考試離現在還很久
B. 像數學、科學什麼的　D. 可是想到還有時間

B In groups of three, practice reading out the above conversation. Next, exchange roles and repeat the exercise.

歷史考試

LESSON 2

zhuàn jì	nián dài	shì jiàn	dài biǎo
傳記	年代	事件	代表 (represent)

kē mù	huà xué	zì rán kē xué
科目 (subject)	化學 (chemistry)	自然科學 (natural science)
shēng wù	wù lǐ	wài yǔ
生物 (biology)	物理 (physics)	外語 (foreign language)

zhǔn bèi	tuì bù	fù xí
準備	退步	複習 (review)
kǒu shì	bǐ shì	shí yàn
口試 (oral examination)	筆試 (written examination)	實驗 (experiment)
fēn shù	cū xīn	xì xīn
分數 (grade; score)	粗心 (careless)	細心 (meticulous)

hǎo mèng	è mèng	shuì guò tóu	áo yè	chí dào
好夢	惡夢 (nightmare)	睡過頭 (oversleep)	熬夜 (work late into the night)	遲到 (be late for (school, work, etc.))

New Words

zhuàn jì 傳記	biography	nián dài 年代	era	shì jiàn 事件	event; incident
zhǔn bèi 準備	prepare	tuì bù 退步	fall behind	hǎo mèng 好夢	sweet dream

Guessing Game

1. The teacher divides the class into two groups and prepares a set of word cards. Each group takes turns sending a representative to draw a card from the teacher.
2. Without mentioning any character on the card, the student can state the number of characters in the word, explain the meaning of the word, or provide synonyms/antonyms in order to give clues for other students to guess the word.
3. The team which makes the higher number of correct guesses within a specific time period wins the game.

歷史考試

Reading

Go 700
Text > Reading section

SCENARIO: It's late and 以晴 is still not in bed. Her father wonders why and decides to take a look.

「以晴！十點多了，快去睡覺。」爸爸看見以晴房間的燈還亮著，就走進來。「我們明天要考世界歷史，我已經看了兩遍了，可是還是記不住，我怕明天考不好。」以晴緊張地對爸爸說。

「以晴，❶讀歷史，最重要的是，要知道事件發生的原因和結果，不是看幾遍的問題。」爸爸說：「想一想，事件是什麼時候發生的？為什麼會發生？有什麼結果？如果是妳，妳會怎麼做？」

以晴看見媽媽也進來了，就問媽媽：「媽媽，妳以前當學生時成績很好，妳教教我，要怎麼讀歷史才能考得好？」

「我們以前歷史的考法跟妳現在的考法不一樣，」媽媽說：「那時候，我們要考年代、人名和地名，要背很多遍才記得住。現在不一樣了，老師要你們寫出自己的看法，所以只要弄懂了事件發生的原因和結果，就可以回答問題了。」

「哪一種考歷史的方法好呢?」以晴問。「像考年代、人名和地名的考法,記性好的人會考得好。像你們這種考歷史的方法,有自己想法的人會考得好。妳喜歡哪一種呢?」爸爸問以晴。

以晴想了想,說:「我不喜歡一直背,❷有些名字和年代,我怎麼背,都背不起來。❸即使記住了,也很快就忘了。我喜歡現在這種考法,可以有自己的看法。」

爸爸說:「以晴,妳喜歡看歷史小說和名人傳記,那些名人故事也是歷史故事,可以幫妳更容易學好歷史。」以晴說:「對啊!我只要把歷史當小說看,再想想那時候的人發生了什麼事,就可以回答問題了。爸爸,媽媽,晚安!祝你們有個好夢!我要去睡了。」

New Words

遍 biàn	(to indicate the number of times an action/state occurs) time	原因 yuán yīn — reason	結果 jié guǒ — result; outcome
看法 kàn fǎ — view; opinion	弄懂 nòng dǒng — having understood	記性 jì xìng — memory	想法 xiǎng fǎ — thought; opinion
即使 jí shǐ — even if	晚安 wǎn ān — good night		

歷史考試

Exercises

True or False?

Answer the questions according to the reading passage.

	對	錯
1. 以晴看了兩遍(biàn)世界歷史了，她不想再看了。	◉	○
2. 以晴的爸爸覺得以晴應該多看幾遍(biàn)課本，記住事件(shì jiàn)的年代(nián dài)、人名和地名。	○	◉
3. 現在考歷史的方法是要學生說出自己的看法(kàn fǎ)。	◉	○
4. 以晴不喜歡只考名字和年代(nián dài)的考試方法。	◉	○
5. 以晴的爸爸覺得歷史也是一種故事。	◉	○

Think & Discuss

Work in pairs and answer the questions in Chinese.

1. 以晴為什麼怕明天的歷史考試會考不好？

2. 媽媽覺得以前和現在考歷史的方法有什麼不一樣？

3. 想考好歷史考試，你覺得什麼最重要？

Culture Link

The Release of Exam Results in Asia

Do you know what the people in the picture are doing? In some Asian countries, academic progression is of utmost importance to students, as good academic results and qualifications lead to better jobs in the future. This culture of emphasizing good academic performance is mainly caused by past societal practices whereby only well-educated scholars can become high-ranking officials and receive a good salary. Hence, even until today, many Asian countries still place a lot of emphasis on examinations, bringing about the 看榜單(kàn bǎngdān, viewing examination results) phenomenon. On the day of the release of examination results, lists of candidates' grades will be displayed in a designated area where students, as well as their concerned parents and friends, can view the results. This explains why the display area is always packed with people trying to view the examination results.

How are examination results usually released in your country?

LESSON 2

1	讀歷史，	最重要的是，	要知道事件發生的原因和結果。
	讀書，		要知道學習的方法。

shì jiàn / yuán yīn / jié guǒ

A: 你知道怎麼準備數學考試嗎？

B: 準備數學考試，最重要的是，把每一個問題弄懂。

nòng dǒng

A: 老師，我想要弄清楚這個自然科學的問題。

zì rán / kē xué

B: 要弄清楚這個問題，最重要的是，把實驗結果記下來。

shí yàn jié guǒ

TIP: When the theme (topic) is placed at the beginning of the sentence, the phrase 最重要的是 can be used to illustrate the main point or technique required to carry out the specific action in accordance with the theme. The speaker speaks with an emphatic or instructive tone.

 **PRACTICE IT** — Using sentence structure 1, complete the dialogues with the helping phrases.

1. A: 考試的時候，我要注意什麼？

   B: _____

2. A: 你覺得要怎麼樣才能交到朋友呢？

   B: _____

3. A: 去海邊玩要注意什麼嗎？

   B: _____

注意天氣的好壞和個人安全／要細心／常常關心他們

xì xīn

歷史考試

2

有些名字和年代，	我	怎麼	背	都	背不下來。
有些中國字，	學生		記		記不住。

年代 nián dài

A: 你還記得小時候的事情嗎？
B: 我的記性不好，我**怎麼**想**都**想不起來。

記性 jì xìng

A: 要拿去拍賣的東西你已經整理好了嗎？
B: 還沒有。有一些東西，我**怎麼**找**都**找不到。

> **TIP** The part after the word 都 describes the situation where the speaker fails to achieve the target despite putting in his or her best. The speaker speaks with a sense of helplessness.

 Using sentence structure 2, complete the dialogues with the helping phrases.

1. A: 你看起來很累，昨天晚上又做惡夢了嗎？
   B: 對啊！我最近常常做惡夢，_____
   _____

   惡夢 è mèng

2. A: 你吃完午餐了嗎？
   B: 還沒有，_____
   _____

3. A: 你是不是忘了我的生日了？
   B: 當然沒有，_____
   _____

Group A　　　　　　　　　　　　　　　　　**Group B**

買太多了／夢裡發生的事／生日和我同一天　→　忘不了／想不起來／吃不完

夢 mèng

22　歷史考試

LESSON 2

3	即使 (jí shǐ)	都記住了，	也	很快就忘了。
		不常考試，		應該要常常練習。

A: 這些化學(huà xué)題目你不是已經懂了嗎？
B: **即使**(jí shǐ)弄懂(nòng dǒng)了，**也**要再練習幾遍(biàn)，才會更清楚。

A: 我昨天複習(fù xí)數學到很晚才睡，可是今天還是考不好。
B: 數學要每天練習，**即使**(jí shǐ)你熬夜(áo yè)，**也**不一定會有好成績。

TIP The conjunction 即使 introduces a hypothetical situation or condition; the outcome stated after 也 will remain unchanged even if the earlier situation or condition has changed.

 Using sentence structure 3, complete the dialogues with the helping phases.

1. A: 我把所有歷史事件(shì jiàn)都背下來了，為什麼還是考不好？

   B: _____

2. A: 我想去遠一點的地方游泳。

   B: 小心一點，_____

3. A: 看你工作這麼累，今天就別出去運動了。

   B: _____

Group A
很會游泳
弄清楚每一個歷史事件(shì jiàn)
工作再累

Group B
有自己的想法(xiǎng fǎ)
找時間運動
要注意安全

Go 700 WANT TO LEARN MORE?
Check out the Text > Sentence Pattern section on the Go700 CD-ROM.

歷史考試

Listening

Text > Dialogue section

SCENARIO: 以晴 and 以安 are both in the study, but it is completely silent inside. Their mother decides to check on them.

 Listen to the Go700 CD-ROM for the dialogue and answer the following multiple-choice questions.

1. 為什麼以晴的數學不太好？
   - (A) 她最近上課不太認真。
   - (B) 她沒時間準備(zhǔn bèi)功課。
   - (C) 她學數學的方法不對。

2. 為什麼以安的數學很好？
   - (A) 他把問題都背下來。
   - (B) 他把老師說的都弄懂(nòng dǒng)了。
   - (C) 他常常問別人。

3. 哪一個學中國字的方法<u>不是</u>老師和媽媽告訴以晴的？
   - (A) 看歷史故事 (B) 看圖說話 (C) 有邊讀邊

4. 聽起來誰的中文比較好？
   - (A) 以安 (B) 以晴 (C) 都不好

5. 下面哪一個句子是對的？
   - (A) 以安的數學退步(tuì bù)了，所以媽媽要他問以晴。
   - (B) 以晴的數學不是不好，是因為沒有弄懂(nòng dǒng)。
   - (C) 以晴把媽媽說的話忘了，所以中國字怎麼背都背不起來。

New Words

難怪 (nán guài) | no wonder

LESSON 2

B Number the following text in the correct order to form a coherent conversation.

[2] 以晴：媽媽，妳快來幫幫我。下個星期就要考數學了，我上課的時候很認真，功課也做了，<ins>可是我就是弄不懂</ins>（nòng dǒng）。好不容易把這題弄懂了，下一題又錯了，怎麼辦？

[8] 以安：我怎麼把媽媽說過的話給忘了？有了方法就不用背，這樣學中國字<ins>又快又有趣</ins>，謝謝以晴。

[1] 媽媽：以安、以晴，你們都在看書啊？

[6] 媽媽：以晴，那妳是怎麼學中國字的呢？

[3] 媽媽：以安，你的數學好，你是怎麼學的，能不能把你的方法告訴以晴？

[5] 以晴：原來是這樣啊！難怪（nán guài）我的數學學不好，<ins>原來是＿＿＿＿＿</ins>，謝謝以安。

[7] 以晴：老師和媽媽都說過，學中國字有「＿＿＿＿＿＿」、「看圖說話」和「＿＿＿＿＿＿」的方法。我覺得學中國字很有趣，知道方法學起來就很容易。

[4] 以安：我也是認真聽老師上課，不過我一定會＿＿＿＿＿＿＿＿＿＿，不懂的再去問別人。我覺得數學很有趣，不像中國字，要一個一個字記，＿＿＿＿＿＿＿＿＿＿。

C Listen to the dialogue on the Go700 CD-ROM again, and fill in the blanks.

歷史考試

Culture Link

In Asia, many students will try to visit temples before their examinations to pray for good results, or successful entry into the school of their choice. They will prepare plenty of offerings before visiting the temple, with the primary aim of putting their minds at ease, so that they can concentrate on the exams afterwards. These offerings are either symbolic in nature, or have similar pronunciations with other auspicious Chinese words.

gāo bǐng　　　　　　gāo　　shēng
糕餅　➡　步步高（糕）升
(cakes or pastries)　(gradual promotion)

suàn tóu　　　　　jīng　jì suàn　suàn
蒜頭　➡　精於計算（蒜）
(garlic)　(to be good at mathematical calculations)

zhú sǔn　　　　　shùn　sǔn　lì
竹筍　➡　順（筍）利，出一節高一節
(bamboo shoots)　(to become successful)　(to symbolize rising through the ranks like the trunks of bamboo)

zòng zi　　　　　bāo zhòng　zòng
粽子　➡　包中（粽）
(rice dumplings)　(to excel in exams)

TALK ABOUT IT In your country, what objects have pronunciations that sound similar to words for being successful in exams?

Role Playing

Form groups of four and role-play the scenario. You may use the sentence structures provided below.

CHARACTERS:

媽媽, 以安, 以晴, 以思

SCENARIO:
The children have received the results of their math exam. 孫媽媽 is talking to her children to find out about their results and learning progress.

SENTENCE STRUCTURES:

1. ……，……怎麼……都……

2. ……，像……什麼的

3. ……，最重要的是，……

4. 即使……，也……
   jí shǐ

LESSON 2

Learn about the Chinese Language & Culture

　　如果有一個工作很多人都想做，就得想方法找到最好的人來做。為了要讓大家都覺得很*公平，所以想出了「考試」這個方法，用考試的方法找人做事。

　　每個來考試的人會得到自己的*分數，有了分數，就可以排出*名次，需要多少人，就從最高分的往下數。如果一次需要二十個人，前二十個高分的人就可以被選上。被選上的人，我們就稱為「*上榜」，「榜」就是寫上*中選者名字的地方。

　　有很多跟考試有關的*成語，像是希望別人考得好，我們可以說「*榜上有名」、「*金榜題名」（*名單上有你的名字）。我們也可以說「*高分中榜」、「*高中榜首」（希望你不但上榜，而且得高分，「榜首」就是第一名的意思）。

*公平 fair　　分數 score　　名次 ranking　　上榜 to be among the top students　　中選者 candidates who have passed the selection criteria
成語 Chinese idiom　　榜上有名 / 金榜題名 to be listed among the top and successful candidates
高分中榜 / 高中榜首 to be ranked high; be the most successful candidate　　名單 name list

歷史考試

Work It Out

There are different types of learning styles, such as visual, auditory, tactile, kinesthetic, etc. Which type of learning style suits you most? What learning strategies or methods will you and your classmate adopt for preparing for your favorite academic subject and activity?

TASK

Survey: Preparing for Your Favorite Subject and Activity

1. The teacher instructs students to cut out the survey form on page 159.
2. Students write down their favorite academic subject and activity, and the learning strategies or methods they adopt.
3. In turns, students share their learning strategies or methods they adopt for preparing for their favorite subject and carrying out their favorite activity.
4. Write down the learning strategies adopted by other classmates that you find suitable and wish to try out.
5. Categorize all the learning strategies and methods adopted by all students into the various learning styles. For each learning style, how many students adopt it? Which is the most popular learning style?

LEARNING LOG

I can...

1. describe my learning experience. ○ ○ ○ ○
2. use "……，最重要的是，……" to illustrate the main point or technique required to carry out a specific action. ○ ○ ○ ○
3. use "……，……怎麼……都……" to describe the situation of failing to achieve the target despite having put in one's best. ○ ○ ○ ○
4. use "即使……，也……" to describe situations or conditions that will not change. ○ ○ ○ ○
5. introduce the exam culture in Asia and state a Chinese idiom associated with exams. ○ ○ ○ ○
6. write 歷史, 傳記, 即使, and 結果. ○ ○ ○ ○

歷史考試

LESSON 3

校外教學
A Field Trip

1. What are these students doing?
2. Have you been to any school field trip before? Do you like it? Why?

My Goals

1. State the preparations to make and the things to note with regard to a school field trip
2. Describe doing things in sequence
3. Repeatedly remind and urge a person to do something
4. Refute a certain viewpoint or give opposing views
5. Understand the history of a compass
6. Understand how Chinese words can be formed through a combination of different characters

Get Started

A Complete the sentences with the sentence structures provided, and arrange them in the correct order to form a coherent story.

6 雖然這個國家公園以晴已經來過幾次了,可是她還是覺得非常有趣。__B__ 要她再來一次,她__B__願意。

1 今天以晴的老師帶全班到國家公園參觀。國家公園__F__學校很遠,開車需要兩個半小時。

2 老師介紹了國家公園。之後,以晴把這裡的風景都畫下來,__D__可愛的小動物、高高的大樹、藍藍的天_____。

5 大家參觀了一天,都有點累了。以晴覺得累一點沒關係,因為來到國家公園,_____,能玩得開心和學到新的東西。

3 可是國家公園有很多有趣的東西,她__A__畫__A__畫不完。

4 午餐過後,老師帶全班一起參觀國家公園。同學們__E__認識了國家公園的歷史,__E__拍了不少照片。

A. ……,……怎麼……都……
B. 即使……,也……
C. ……,最重要的是,……
D. ……,像……什麼的
E. 不但……,還……
F. ……離……

LESSON 3

Vocabulary Builder

jì niàn pǐn	jì niàn rì
紀念品 (souvenir)	紀念日 (anniversary)

jì niàn bēi	jì niàn guǎn
紀念碑 (monument)	紀念館 (memorial hall)

shī / shī shī de	fáng huá	yǔ yī
濕/濕濕的 (wet)	防滑 (prevent slippery)	雨衣 (raincoat)

gān / gān gān de	yǔ xié
乾/乾乾的 (dry)	雨鞋 (rain boots)

shài shāng	fáng shài	fáng shài yóu
晒傷 (sunburnt)	防晒	防晒油 (sunscreen lotion)

tài yáng yǎn jìng	hù wài	wén chóng
太陽眼鏡 (sunglasses)	戶外 (outdoors)	蚊蟲 (mosquitoes and insects)

yě cān	jiāo yóu
野餐 (picnic)	郊遊 (excursion)

xīng fèn	shī wàng
興奮 (excited)	失望 (to feel disappointed)

qí dài
期待 (look forward; yearn)

New Words

jì niàn pǐn 紀念品 — souvenir	shī / shī shī de 濕/濕濕的 — wet	fáng huá 防滑 — anti-slip
yǔ yī 雨衣 — raincoat	shài shāng 晒傷 — sunburnt	fáng shài 防晒 — sunscreen
fáng shài yóu 防晒油 — sunscreen lotion	xīng fèn 興奮 — excited	

New Words Roll Call

1. Teacher gives students one minute to memorize all the new words.
2. Each student draws nine squares on a piece of blank paper, and fills in the squares with nine words that they have memorized.
3. Teacher reads out the new words (or instruct any student to take turns and read out the new words) while students circle the corresponding words in the squares.
4. The first student who circles all nine words and is able to accurately pronounce them wins the game.

校外教學

Reading

SCENARIO: 以思 has a special home assignment today. The teacher will bring the class for a field trip next Monday, and the students are to list the items they need to bring for the trip. When 以思 reaches home, he starts to discuss with his mother.

下星期一，以思的老師要帶大家去校外教學(xiào wài jiào xué)，他們要在船(chuán)上上課，每個學生聽了，都興奮(xīng fèn)得不得了。老師說：「今天的功課就是，①把下星期一要帶的東西一樣一樣寫出來。」

以思拿了一張紙和一枝筆，一邊想，一邊寫下他應該帶的東西：

1. 三明治、點心和糖果(táng guǒ)
2. 相機
3. 買紀念品(jì niàn pǐn)的錢

媽媽看了他寫的單子，說：「可以帶一點錢，可是，不一定是買紀念品(jì niàn pǐn)的。還有呢？」以思說：「我想不出來還要帶什麼東西。」媽媽說：「船(chuán)上風很大，不需要帶外套嗎？海上太陽大，容易(róng yì)晒傷(shài shāng)，要不要帶帽子，還有防晒油(fáng shài yóu)？」以思聽了，又把這些東西加上去了。

「你只記得帶吃的東西，怎麼忘了帶喝的呢？還有，在船(chuán)上容易弄濕(shī)，最好穿防滑(fáng huá)、防水(fáng shuǐ)的鞋子，還要帶雨衣(yǔ yī)，相機也要小心拿好。」媽媽說。

LESSON 3

媽媽又問：「到了船(chuán)上，要注意什麼？」以思回答：「要注意聽老師講課(jiǎng kè)。」「對！」媽媽接著說：「記得跟同學走在一起。記住安全第一，不可以和同學在船(chuán)上跑來跑去，船(chuán)上地滑，容易摔倒受傷。還有船(chuán)會搖來搖去，要小心，❷千萬(qiān wàn)別掉(diào)到海裡去了。」

「要注意的事情怎麼那麼多？」以思說。「這些本來就是校外教學(xiào wài jiào xué)要注意的事情啊！」媽媽說：「對了，別忘了帶筆和本子，把老師介紹的海洋生物(hǎi yáng shēng wù)，牠們的名字、吃的東西，還有怎麼生活都記下來、照下來。回來以後，再把照片、筆記(bǐ jì)整理出來，這樣才能真正學到東西。」

以思說：「真麻煩(má fán)！我還以為校外教學(xiào wài jiào xué)就是出去玩呢！」媽媽回答：「校外教學(xiào wài jiào xué)是到不同的地方學習，是又好玩又有趣的經驗。如果你們不好好地照顧自己、注意安全，才是給老師找麻煩(má fán)呢！」

New Words

校外教學 (xiào wài jiào xué)	field trip	船 (chuán)	boat; ship	糖果 (táng guǒ)	candy
防水 (fáng shuǐ)	waterproof	講課 (jiǎng kè)	conduct lessons	千萬 (qiān wàn)	be sure to
掉 (diào)	fall; drop	海洋 (hǎi yáng)	ocean	生物 (shēng wù)	organism
筆記 (bǐ jì)	notes	麻煩 (má fán)	troublesome; be a bother		

校外教學

Exercises

Think & Write

Below are the situations that 以思 may encounter during the field trips. Write down the items 以思 may need to prepare in order to prevent them from happening.

要準備的東西：雨衣和防滑

要準備的東西：防油巾帽子太陽

要準備的東西：三明治點心和口喝

要準備的東西：筆、本子和相本

Think & Discuss

Work in pairs and answer the questions in Chinese.

1. 老師給以思的功課是什麼？

2. 以思去校外教學應該要注意什麼？
   xiào wài jiào xué

3. 你以前去過哪些地方校外教學？你帶了哪些東西？
   xiào wài jiào xué

Language Focus

LESSON 3

1	把	下星期要帶的東西	一樣一樣（地）	寫出來。
		明天要交的作業	一題一題（地）	做完。

A: 你的字寫得真好，真漂亮！
B: 老師要我們把字一個一個（地）寫清楚。

A: 我怕我寫不完這些明信片。
B: 我們還有四個小時，可以把這些明信片一張一張（地）寫完。

TIP: The structure " 一 + Measure Word + 一 + Measure Word (地) + Verb Phrase" means that an action is not completed in a single session, and has to be done in sequence. The adverb 地 after the second measure word can be omitted in the sentence/text.

PRACTICE IT

Using sentence structure 1, complete the dialogues with the helping phrases.

1. A: 這本相簿是你去校外教學時照的嗎？（xiào wài jiào xué）
   B: 對，我 __把校外__

2. A: 老師說這些海洋生物考試都會考。（hǎi yáng shēng wù）
   B: 那我得 __把海洋生物一__

3. A: 我的衣服太多了，櫃子看起來真亂！
   B: 你應該 __把衣__

Group A	Group B
件	整理好
(個)	(掛起來)
張	記下來

校外教學

2. 千萬(qiān wàn)
| 別 | 掉到海裡去了。 |
| 別 | 忘了帶筆和本子。 |

TIP: 千萬 indicates a tone of repeated reminders, while 別/不要/不可以 means to forbid or to advise against doing something. Hence, the structure "千萬別/不要/不可以……" is used to indicate that certain actions or things should not be done.

A: 你怎麼把哥哥心愛的玩具弄壞了？
B: 千萬(qiān wàn)不要告訴哥哥！

A: 今天下課以後，我和妹妹要一起去紀念館(jì niàn guǎn)。
B: 好，注意安全，千萬(qiān wàn)不可以太晚回家。

 Complete the dialogues using sentence structure 2.

1. A: 今天晚上我要和同學去欣賞音樂會。
   B: 晚上比較冷，記得帶外套，千_____

2. A: 明天的考試我已經準備好了。
   B: 老師說這次考試題目很多，_____

3. A: 我們打算下個月要去野餐(yě cān)。
   B: 我也想要去，到時候千萬別忘了_____

4. A: 我明天就要搭飛機去旅行了。
   B: 千萬_____

LESSON 3

Listening

Text > Dialogue section

SCENARIO: It's time for class, but 以思 and his classmates are not in the classroom.

A Listen to the Go700 CD-ROM for the dialogue and answer the following multiple-choice questions.

1. 老師在哪裡跟學生說話？　　**C**
   (A) chuán 船上　(B) chuán 船邊　(C) 學校裡

2. chuán 上船以後應該先做什麼？　　**C**
   (A) 看yú fū漁夫工作　(B) 聽老師說話　(C) 穿jiù shēng yī救生衣

3. 以思穿jiù shēng yī救生衣的時候，同學為什麼笑他？　　**C**
   (A) 以思不會穿jiù shēng yī救生衣。
   (B) 以思穿jiù shēng yī救生衣看起來像yú fū漁夫。
   (C) 以思穿jiù shēng yī救生衣看起來胖胖的。

4. 要上chuán船了，學生怎麼樣？　　**A**
   (A) 很xīng fèn興奮　(B) 很聽話　(C) 很緊張

5. 下面哪一個句子是對的？　　**B**
   (A) 以思等一下要帶同學到chuán船邊看yú fū漁夫工作。
   (B) 這是以思最後一次到大chuán船上，所以很xīng fèn興奮。
   (C) 老師希望學生穿上並檢查自己的jiù shēng yī救生衣。

New Words

yú fū 漁夫	fisherman	jiù shēng yī 救生衣	life jacket
gǎn kuài 趕快	hurry	dāng xīn 當心	be careful of

校外教學

B Number the following text in the correct order to form a coherent conversation.

[5] 以思：❸你才是大胖子呢！

[1] 老師：各位同學，請注意！到船(chuán)上以後，請大家小心(xiǎo xīn)，不要 <u>在船上跑來跑去</u> 當心(dāng xīn)滑倒摔傷了！

[7] 以思：老師，對不起，這是我第一次到這麼大的船(chuán)上來，<u>我太興奮</u>了。

[2] 以思：老師，我們可以到船(chuán)邊看漁夫(yú fū)工作嗎？

[6] 老師：你們不要吵了！趕快(gǎn kuài) <u>檢查一下</u> 自己的救生(jiù shēng)衣(yī)穿好了沒？

[4] 同學：(同學們上船(chuán)後)以思，你穿救生衣(jiù shēng yī)的樣子真好笑，<u>又胖又圓</u>的，<u>像個大胖</u>！

[8] 老師：各位同學，拿好你們的東西，小心地跟著我，我們要去看漁夫(yú fū)工作了。

[3] 老師：等一下老師再帶你們去看，你們不可以自己過去，<u>太危險了</u>！還有上船(chuán)以後，會發給大家救生衣(jiù shēng yī)，大家記得把救生衣(jiù shēng yī)穿好。

C Listen to the dialogue on the Go700 CD-ROM again, and fill in the blanks.

校外教學

LESSON 3

3	你	才	是大胖子呢！
	如果你們不注意安全，		是給老師找麻煩(má fán)。

A: 住在小城裡，我覺得交通很不方便。

B: 大城市車子和人都很多，去哪裡都要很久，才不方便呢！

TIP The word 才 indicates a tone of emphasis and certainty. When another person expresses his or her views, 才 can be used as a rebuttal to that viewpoint.

A: 我覺得冬天下雨的時候好冷。

B: 冬天會下雪的國家，才讓人冷得受不了呢！ (shou)

 Using sentence structure 3, complete the dialogues with the helping phrases.

1. A: 搭火車去北部真方便。
   B: 我覺得 搭飛機去北部才方便 （搭飛機）

2. A: 假日的時候在家休息最舒服。
   B: 假日去公園野餐才舒服 （去公園野餐 yě cān）

3. A: 大商場裡什麼都有，很有意思。
   B: 可是 小商店有各國的東西小店才有意思 （小商店有各國的東西）

Check out the Text > Sentence Pattern section on the Go700 CD-ROM.

校外教學

The Compass

Do you know what this is? This is the earliest form of compass known as 司南 (sīnán). People in ancient China discovered that magnetic metals possess the properties of magnetic attraction, and are able to point to the direction of north and south. Hence, they invented the earliest compass, 司南. By the Song dynasty, the ancient Chinese made a compass that was easier to operate, fixed it on a plate marked with directional bearings, and named it 羅盤 (luópán). The invention was soon adopted by seafarers to be used in navigation. By the end of the 11th century, the widespread use of compasses made it one of the most important tools for navigation between different countries.

 Are there any great inventions in your country? Which one is your favorite? Why?

Form groups of three and role-play the scenario. You may use the sentence structures provided below.

CHARACTERS:

媽媽, 以晴, 以思

SCENARIO:

以思 is going on a school field trip tomorrow. He is getting ready the necessary things to bring along and his mother is constantly reminding him of the things that he needs to take note of.

SENTENCE STRUCTURES:

1. ……才……
2. qiān wàn
   千萬……
3. 不但……，還……
4. ……，最重要的是，……
5. 一 + Measure Word + 一 + Measure Word (地) + Verb Phrase

校外教學

LESSON 3

Learn about the Chinese Language & Culture

　　漢字*組合真的很有趣，用*獨立的字可以組合成不同意思的字。像是「日」和「西」就可以組合成「*晒」。

　　你可以從學過的字中找到很多這種有趣的組合，像是「日、月」為「明」，「女、子」為「好」，「田、力」為「男」，「田、心」為「思」，「合、手」為「拿」。除了兩個字的組合，還有三個字的組合，像是「馬、大、可」為「*騎」，「言、身、寸」為「謝」。

　　以前的人，利用字組合的*特性，寫出不同的句子或*文章。有時候在一些慶祝活動上，也會有*猜字謎的活動。簡單的字謎像是「十一口」，*謎底是「吉」。*比較難的像是「早生二十四小時」，謎底是「天」（大一天，「天」是「大」和「一」的組合）。「有人在家嗎？」，謎底是「問」（門口問，「問」是「門」和「口」的組合）。

---

*組合 combination; combine　　獨立 independent　　晒 shine upon; dry sth. in the sun　　騎 ride　　特性 characteristic
文章 essay; article　　猜字謎 solve a riddle / puzzle　　謎底 answer to a riddle / puzzle　　比較 relatively

校外教學

Work It Out

Where do you want to go for your school field trip? Have you been to any tourist attractions that you would like to introduce to your classmates? Plan a field trip with your classmates, and list the things to take note of.

Proposing a Field Trip

1. Split the students into 3 groups; each group will write down the place that they want to go for their field trip.
2. Discuss the reasons for selecting that place and the activities that can be carried out there. List the estimated expenses, transportation options, time needed, as well as areas requiring parents' collaboration.
3. After the discussion, each group will compile their results and come up with a field trip proposal.
4. Each group will send a representative to present their proposal, and the class will vote for the field trip they like most.

LEARNING LOG

I can...

		Excellent	Good	Fair	Need Improvement
1	describe the details to take note of and things to prepare for a school field trip.	○	○	○	○
2	use "一 + Measure Word + 一 + Measure Word (地) + Verb Phrase" to refer to doing things in sequence.	○	○	○	○
3	use "千萬……" to repeatedly remind and urge a person to do something.	○	○	○	○
4	use "……才……" to rebut another person's opinion.	○	○	○	○
5	form three Chinese words by combining different Chinese characters.	○	○	○	○
6	write 船, 興奮, 防晒, and 紀念品.	○	○	○	○

LESSON 4

退休生活
Life after Retirement

1. What are these elderly doing? Are they still working?
2. What kind of life do you think these elderly are leading?

My Goals

1. Understand the similarities and differences between Eastern and Western perspectives on retirement
2. Express opinions from someone else's perspective
3. State a hypothetical situation to ask for other people's opinion
4. Provide options in a question and make a conclusion based on what has been said
5. Understand the differences between Eastern and Western perspectives on living with extended families
6. Understand and appreciate the form of Chinese seven-character-quatrain poems

SCENARIO: 以晴 visits 白爺爺 and sees him busy in his room.

A Fill in the blanks with the appropriate options below.

以　晴：白爺爺，您在做什麼？

白爺爺：我在整理房間。真是不好意思，到處都是書。

以　晴：沒關係，讓我幫您把這些書_____B_____！

白爺爺：謝謝！這些本來就是我要做的事，不過有妳的幫忙，___A___。

以　晴：白爺爺，您覺得現在的生活好不好？

白爺爺：好是好，_____D_____，還好我有很多朋友。

以　晴：要是您覺得無聊，___C___，我可以帶您去欣賞音樂會、吃美食。

白爺爺：謝謝妳，以晴。有妳這個朋友，我的生活更有趣了！

A. 我才可以休息一下　　C. 千萬別忘了我
B. 一本一本放好吧　　　D. 可是有時候覺得很無聊

B In pairs, practice reading out the above conversation. Next, exchange roles and repeat the exercise.

退休生活

LESSON 4

Vocabulary Builder

tuì xiū	tuì xiū jīn	dú zì	gū dān
退休	退休金 (pension)	獨自 (alone)	孤單 (lonely)

yǎng lǎo yuàn	dān dú	péi bàn
養老院 (nursing home; old folks' home)	單獨 (alone; solitary)	陪伴 (accompany)

rěn nài	rěn xīn	gù xiāng	pá shān	nóng cūn
忍耐 (tolerate; endure)	忍心 (be hardhearted enough to)	故鄉	爬山	農村 (farm)

rěn ràng	rěn bú zhù	sēn lín	hú pàn
忍讓 (forbear)	忍不住 (unable to bear; cannot help (doing sth.))	森林 (forest)	湖畔 (lakeside)

shú xī	mò shēng	zì yóu	jū shù
熟悉 ⇄ 陌生 (strange; unfamiliar)		自由 (free) ⇄ 拘束 (feel restricted)	

dú lì	yī lài	jiē jìn	yuǎn lí
獨立 ⇄ 依賴 (rely on)		接近 (close) ⇄ 遠離 (far apart)	

New Words

tuì xiū	gù xiāng	pá shān	shú xī	dú lì
退休 | retire	故鄉 | hometown	爬山 | mountain climbing	熟悉 | familiar	獨立 | independent

Protect the Fortress

1. Students are each given a word card and they have to sit in a row.
2. Besides memorizing the word card that they have, students have to memorize the word cards held by their classmates to their left and right.
3. The teacher picks and reads out a word from the cards. The student holding on to that particular word card remains seated but the two students beside him/her have to stand up.
4. The slower student, or the students who stand up when they are not supposed to will lose a point each, and they have to remain standing until they construct a sentence with the word on their word card.
5. Depending on the situation, the teacher can let the students swap their cards, or let a student hold two cards at one time.

退休生活

Reading

SCENARIO: Sunny's (以晴) grandparents have retired and her family is talking about their retirement plans.

以晴的爺爺奶奶一直住在美國北方。今年，爺爺退休了，他們決定把房子賣了，搬到南方來。

「爸爸，」以晴問：「他們為什麼想搬到南方來呢？」

「年紀大的人都怕冷，都喜歡陽光。美國那麼大，多住幾個不同的地方也是很有趣的。」爸爸回答。

「媽媽，」以安問：「外公外婆退休以後會不會搬家呢？」媽媽說：「他們喜歡和家人一起住在熟悉的地方。所以外公外婆退休後，還是會住在原來的地方。」「外公外婆不怕冷嗎？」以安說：「就像爺爺奶奶那樣。」

「❶很冷、很熱，對外公外婆來說，都是可以忍受的。能和家人住在一起，又有老朋友住在附近，平常可以說說話，可以互相照顧，這才是最重要的。」媽媽說。

「外公外婆不願意住在不同的地方嗎？」以安問。媽媽說：「外公外婆常常出國旅行，可是退休(tuì xiū)以後，他們不願意搬到一個天氣好，卻沒有家人和朋友的地方。」

以晴說：「真奇怪，爺爺奶奶和外公外婆都是老人(lǎo rén)，可是他們的想法卻差(chā)那麼多。」媽媽說：「是啊！不同國家的人或是在不同地方長大的人，會有不同的想法。有些老人(lǎo rén)比較(bǐ jiào)獨立(dú lì)，有些老人(lǎo rén)比較(bǐ jiào)喜歡和親人住在一起。」

「那麼，以後妳跟爸爸退休(tuì xiū)了，你們怎麼辦？」以思問：「你們是不同國家的人，妳要回妳的故鄉(gù xiāng)去，他要去有太陽的地方，怎麼辦？」爸爸說：「很容易啊！媽媽老了，喜歡回到故鄉(gù xiāng)去；我老了，喜歡去一個新地方。我可以跟媽媽回她的故鄉(gù xiāng)去，這不是很好嗎？」

New Words

年紀 nián jì — age	平常 píng cháng — usual	互相 hù xiāng — mutually / each other	老人 lǎo rén — elderly
差 chā — difference	比較 bǐ jiào — quite; relatively / compare	忍受 rěn shòu — tolerate	

退休生活

Exercises

True or False?

Answer the questions according to the reading passage.

	對	錯
1. 以晴的爺爺奶奶本來住在美國南方。	○	✗
2. 以晴的外公外婆退休(tuì xiū)後還是想住在原來的地方。	✓	○
3. 以晴的外公外婆不怕冷。	✓	✓
4. 以晴的爺爺奶奶跟外公外婆的想法不一樣。	✓	○
5. 以晴的爸媽退休(tuì xiū)以後，兩個人會搬到不一樣的地方住。	○	✓

Think & Discuss

Work in pairs and answer the questions in Chinese.

1. 以晴的爺爺奶奶和外公外婆退休(tuì xiū)後想住的地方有什麼不一樣？你比較(bǐ jiào)喜歡哪一個地方？

2. 以晴的爸爸媽媽退休(tuì xiū)之後想要住在哪裡？

3. 你的爺爺奶奶和外公外婆退休(tuì xiū)了嗎？說說他們的退休(tuì xiū)生活。

Culture Link

The Place to Retire

Western people usually choose a place to retire, which may not be their hometown. However, to some Chinese people, even if they have established their career and family in a foreign country, by the time they retire, their biggest wish is to return to their hometown. This is because they are familiar with the local customs and culture, since it was the place they spent their childhood years. Therefore, some Chinese people see their hometown as the best place to spend their old age.

1. Where do you want to live when you retire? Why?
2. Interview your classmates to find out where they would like to live when they retire and the reason why.

退休生活

LESSON 4

Language Focus

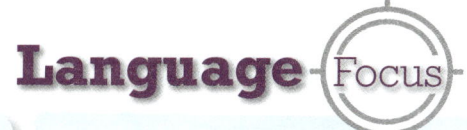

1

| 很冷、很熱， | 對 | 外公外婆 | 來說， | 都是可以忍受的。(rěn shòu) |
| 數學， | 對 | 以安 | 來說， | 是很有意思的。 |

A: 歷史要背很多人名和年代，很麻煩。
B: 學歷史，對我來說，就像看故事書一樣有趣。

A: 住在小城，上班、上學、買東西方便嗎？
B: 對有車子的人來說，交通不是問題。

> **TIP** The structure "對……來說，……" is to express the opinion of another person from his/her perspective. The subject after 對 is the person the speaker is referring to. Generally, this structure is located at the beginning of a sentence, though it can also be placed after the topic.

 **PRACTICE IT** Using sentence structure 1, complete the dialogues with the helping phrases.

1. A: 這個紀念品不便宜，但我還是忍不住想要買回家。(rěn bú zhù)
   B: 對光客來說旅行買的紀念品一也沒係

2. A: 父母退休以後要做什麼呢？(tuì xiū)
   B: 對父母來說回到的故看老朋友， ， 才是他們想要過的退休生活。(tuì xiū)

3. A: 明天的考試你已經準備好了，還擔心什麼？
   B: 對我來說考試讓我得不張

Group A	Group B
我	回到熟悉的故鄉看看老朋友 (shú xī / gù xiāng)
觀光客	紀念品貴一點也沒關係
父母	考試讓人緊張得睡不著

退休生活

Listening

Text > Dialogue section

SCENARIO: 以晴 is about to go out when she saw 以思 sitting in the backyard looking troubled. She approaches him to find out what is wrong.

 Listen to the Go700 CD-ROM for the dialogue and answer the following multiple-choice questions.

1. 以思在煩惱什麼？
   (A) 他退休(tuì xiū)後要做什麼。
   (B) 他退休(tuì xiū)後要住在哪裡。
   (C) 他退休(tuì xiū)後跟誰一起住。

2. 以思不喜歡住在哪裡？
   (A) 南方 (B) 溫暖的地方 (C) 離家人和朋友很遠的地方

3. 以晴覺得以思應該住在哪裡？
   (A) 他喜歡的地方
   (B) 跟她住在同一個社區
   (C) 交通方便的地方

4. 以思不煩惱了，他和以晴要去做什麼？
   (A) 去操場跑步 (B) 去爬(pá)山(shān) (C) 去公園玩飛(fēi)盤(pán)

5. 下面哪一個句子是對的？
   (A) 以晴和以思都喜歡南方的風景和陽光。
   (B) 以晴覺得現在的世界像個小社區，到哪裡都方便。
   (C) 以思早就知道可以坐飛機去找以晴了。

New Words

飛盤 (fēi pán) | flying disc; Frisbee

LESSON 4

B Number the following text in the correct order to form a coherent conversation.

[4] 以思：我很喜歡<u>南方的風景和陽光</u>，可是我也喜歡跟家人、朋友住在一起。②要是你們跟朋友都搬到很遠的地方去，我該怎麼辦？

[2] 以思：我在煩惱(fán nǎo)。我在想我老了，退休(tuì xiū)以後，③我是<u>留在這裡</u>，還是搬到(bān dào)別的地方去？

[6] 以思：我怎麼沒想到呢？④這麼說，要是你們搬到很遠的地方，我也可以<u>坐飛機去看你們</u>！

[5] 以晴：你想住哪裡就住哪裡啊！再說現在的交通很方便，<u>世界就像一個小社區</u>，即使住在不同的國家，也像住在附近一樣。

[1] 以晴：以思，要不要跟我們<u>一起去公園玩</u>？你一個人坐在這裡在想什麼？

[7] 以晴：現在不擔心了吧！

[8] 以思：謝謝妳，我們<u>一起去公園</u>玩飛盤(fēi pán)吧！

[3] 以晴：原來你在想這件事(zhè jiàn shì)啊！

C Listen to the dialogue on the Go700 CD-ROM again, and fill in the blanks.

退休生活

2	要是	你們跟朋友都搬到很遠的地方，	（我）	怎麼辦？
		不小心掉到海裡		

A: 要是中秋節天氣不好，看不到月亮，怎麼辦？

B: 看不到月亮沒關係，最重要的是，能跟家人在一起說說笑笑。

TIP The structure "要是……" indicates a hypothetical situation and 怎麼辦 is used to ask for someone's opinion on that situation. The subject can be omitted if the context is clear.

A: 要是我的青春痘好不了，怎麼辦？

B: 只要常洗臉，少吃油的、辣的食物，多喝水，就會好得比較快。

Using sentence structure 2, complete the dialogues with the helping phrases.

1. A: 要是我自出旅行受不了孤，怎麼辦

   B: 你可以打電話給我。

2. A: 要是來不及把東西準備好怎麼辦

   B: 不用擔心，我們一起來幫你，一定能做好的。

3. A: 要是今天一起出去去玩的人太多

   B: 沒關係的，人多一點才好玩呀！

> dú zì　　　　　gū dān
> 獨自出國受不了孤單／來不及把東西準備好／
> 一起出去玩的人太多

退休生活

LESSON 4

3

我	是	留在這裡，
明天你		留在家裡看書，

	搬到別的地方去？
還是	跟朋友去看電影？

TIP The structure is used to form choice-type questions. The word 還是 is placed between two options. Though it is a question, the question word 嗎 should **not** be added at the end of the sentence.

A: 你長大以後**是**想當作家，**還是**想當醫生？
B: 我想當作家，把我的想法都寫出來。

A: 媽媽的禮物**是**要去大商場買，**還是**要去小商店買？
B: 只要能買到我們要送的東西，就去那裡買。

PRACTICE IT Using sentence structure 3, complete the dialogues with the helping phrases.

1. A: 明天你是想去海玩還是留在家 ?
   B: 要看明天的天氣是晴天還是雨天來決定。

2. A: 你是一個獨立的人還是喜依賴別人 ?
   B: 不一定，但是我想成為一個獨立(dú lì)的人。

3. A: 他爸爸是回鄉是去老院了 ?
   B: 聽說他爸爸拿了退休金(tuì xiū jīn)回故鄉(gù xiāng)了。

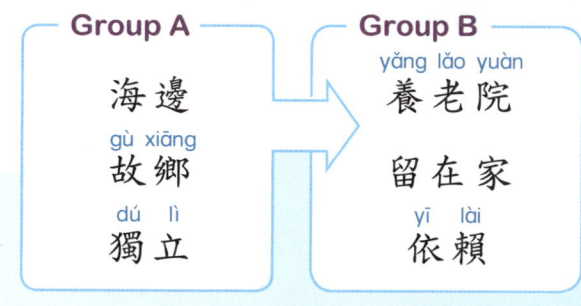

Group A → Group B

海邊 → 養老院 (yǎng lǎo yuàn)
故鄉 (gù xiāng) → 留在家
獨立 (dú lì) → 依賴 (yī lài)

退休生活

| 4 | 這麼說， | 要是你們搬到很遠的地方，我也可以坐飛機去看你們！ |
| | | 我們應該去郊外走走，多接近(jiē jìn)大自然。 |

A: 你看！我昨天去海邊忘了帶防曬油，結果曬傷了。
B: **這麼說**，夏天去海邊最好還是擦防曬油，才不容易曬傷。

> **TIP** After the phrase 這麼說, the speaker makes a conclusion based on what the other party has said.

A: 聽說這次考試的題目不難，都是老師上課教過的。
B: **這麼說**，只要把老師上課教的弄懂，考試就沒問題了。

 Using sentence structure 4, complete the dialogues with the helping phrases.

1. A: 我的爺爺奶奶決定退休(tuì xiū)後搬到鄉下(xiāng xià)住。
   B: 這麼說你的爸爸奶奶比較喜大自然，不喜歡住在大城市。

2. A: 好朋友本來就應該互相(hù xiāng)幫忙。
   B: 這麼說我們應該互相關心

(continued on page 55)

LESSON 4

3. A: 大家都覺得這次歷史考試不難。
   B: 這麼說大家的成績應該都不差。

> 成績應該都不差 (chā)
> 比較喜歡大自然 (bǐ jiào)
> 應該互相關心 (hù xiāng)

WANT TO LEARN MORE?

Check out the Text > Sentence Pattern section on the Go700 CD-ROM.

Culture Link

Living with Extended Families

"三代同堂" (sān dài tóng táng, three generations under one roof) is a traditional form of living arrangement for Chinese extended families. It reflects a closely-knitted and cohesive family unit, where the traditional values of filial piety and clan culture can be passed on to the next generation. Nowadays, other than this form of living arrangement, there is a growing number of young couples who choose to live near their parents instead of living together, in order to strike a balance between privacy and convenience. Alternatively, they may also choose to stay in the same apartment building or within the same estate or district as their parents, to maintain a mutually dependent yet cordial parent-child relationship. In this way, they can take care of each other due to the close proximity, but are still able to lead their own lives without interference.

In the West, it is rare to see three generations living together, and once children reach adulthood, they will usually move out to work in cities, and return only during the holiday seasons to spend time together as a family. Now, due to Western influences as well as urbanization, there are fewer and fewer families with three generations living together in China.

1. According to your own observations, do adults in your country still stay with their parents?
2. Do you want to live with your parents in the future? Why?

退休生活

Role Playing

Form groups of four and role-play the scenario. You may use the sentence structures provided below.

CHARACTERS:

媽媽, 以安, 以晴, 以思

SCENARIO:

以安, 以晴, and 以思 are curious about how their parents will spend their life after retirement. They ask their mother about their retirement plan.

SENTENCE STRUCTURES:

1. ……是……，還是……？
2. 對……來說，……
3. 要是……，怎麼辦？
4. 這麼說，……
5. 千萬……

LESSON 4

Learn about the Chinese Language & Culture

huí xiāng ǒu shū
回鄉偶書
(Returning to My Hometown)

táng　hè zhī zhāng
唐・賀知章

shào xiǎo lí jiā lǎo dà huí
少小離家老大回，
(I left home young, I return old;)

xiāng yīn wú gǎi bìn máo cuī
鄉音無改鬢毛衰，
(My accent remains unchanged, but my hair has turned gray;)

ér tóng xiāng jiàn bù xiāng shì
兒童相見不相識，
(The children, meeting me, do not know me;)

xiào wèn kè cóng hé chù lái
笑問客從何處來。
(They smile and ask, "Sir, where do you come from?")

　　這首詩是*詩人年老後回到故鄉，*遇到一些小朋友，因為小朋友*天真的問話而有很多想法，於是把當時的心情寫下來。

　　詩不容易寫，因為有很多*規定。這一首詩是*七言*絕句。絕句是一首詩有四句，作者把要說的事在四句中說清楚。*五言或七言，是每一句可以用的字數。「回鄉偶書」是七言，就是一句只能有七個字，整首詩只能用二十八個字。

　　你聽過其他五言絕句或是七言絕句嗎？請和你的朋友一起分享。

*詩人 poet　　遇 meet　　天真 naive　　規定 regulation　　七言 seven-character　　絕句 quatrain; a four-line poem
五言 five-character

退休生活

Work It Out

Have you ever thought of the life that you want to lead after you retire? Try to imagine what will happen in 60 years' time and how your life will change, then plan for your own retirement.

TASK
Retirement Planning

1. The class will discuss how life will be like in 60 years' time. What lifestyle changes in food, clothing, accommodation, transportation, education, and leisure do you expect?

2. Write down your daily routine after you retire.

   60年後我＿＿＿＿歲，我一天的生活是：

時間	做什麼事

3. Talk about your retirement lifestyle planning with your classmates, and choose the retirement planning you like most and explain why.

LEARNING LOG

I can...

		Excellent	Good	Fair	Need Improvement
1	state the differences between Eastern and Western perspectives on retirement and on living with extended families.	○	○	○	○
2	use "對……來說，……" to express the opinion from another person's perspective.	○	○	○	○
3	use "要是……，怎麼辦？" to state a hypothetical situation to ask for someone's opinion.	○	○	○	○
4	use "……是……，還是……？" to provide options in a question.	○	○	○	○
5	use "這麼說，……" to make a conclusion based on what has already been said.	○	○	○	○
6	Write 退休, 忍受, 比較, and 獨立.	○	○	○	○

LESSON 5

熱鬧的選舉
The Exciting Election

1. What are these students doing?
2. If there were an election for the student council's president, would you like to be a candidate? Why?

My Goals

1. Know about electoral campaigns and state the prerequisites of an election candidate
2. Express how an item is used at a certain location to complete an action
3. Know how to express the conditions to be fulfilled before a target can be achieved
4. Know how political elections are carried out in different countries
5. Understand how Chinese antitheses are used in sentences

A Fill in the blanks with the appropriate sentence structures to complete the passage.

下個星期學校有一個活動，__不但__要選出幫忙辦校外教學的學生，__還__要選出學校商店的店員。

以思__不但__成績好，大家__也__很喜歡他。所以很多人都覺得_____他參加，一定能被選上。__對__以思__來說__，不管__是__辦校外教學，__還是__當學校商店的店員，他都很有興趣。所以只要有機會，這兩樣工作他都想試一試。

A. 要是……	D. 不但……，還……
B. 不管……	E. 是……，還是……
C. 對……來說	F. 不但……，也……

B In pairs, assuming you are 以思, discuss whether you would rather be a school store assistant or organize extra-curricular activities, and explain why.

LESSON 5

Vocabulary Builder

xuǎn jǔ	jìng xuǎn	tóu / tóu piào	hòu xuǎn rén	fù zé	bāng zhù
選舉 election	競選 campaign	投/投票 vote	候選人 candidate	負責 responsible	幫助 help

dāng xuǎn	luò xuǎn	zhù xuǎn yuán	zhèng jiàn	xié zhù	zhī chí
當選 elected	落選 (lose an election)	助選員 (election agent)	政見 (political view)	協助 (assist)	支持 (support)

rè nào	lěng qīng
熱鬧 lively ⇔ 冷清 (cold and cheerless)

jiǎn dān	fù zá
簡單 simple ⇔ 複雜 (complicated)

gōng zhèng	piān sī
公正 (fair and just) ⇔ 偏私 (partial; unfair)

hǎi bào	tú huà	tú àn	huì lù
海報 poster	圖畫 (drawing)	圖案 (graphics; pattern)	賄賂 (bribe)

lì yì	bù zé shǒu duàn	bǐng gōng wú sī
利益 (interest; benefit)	不擇手段 (resort to unscrupulous means)	秉公無私 (handle matters impartially)

New Words

xuǎn jǔ 選舉	election	jìng xuǎn 競選	contest an election	tóu / tóu piào 投/投票	vote	hòu xuǎn rén 候選人	candidate
dāng xuǎn 當選	be elected	fù zé 負責	be responsible for	bāng zhù 幫助	help	rè nào 熱鬧	crowded and lively
jiǎn dān 簡單	simple	hǎi bào 海報	poster				

Guess the Correct Word

1. The teacher prepares a set of word cards and divides the class into two groups.
2. Each group takes turns to send a representative to the front. The teacher randomly picks a word card, keeps it away from the representative but shows it to other students.
3. Students in the same group as the representative are to provide three related words or sentences as clues. For instance, if the answer is 候選人, students can say the words 選舉, 政見, and 投票 as clues for the representative to guess the word. If the representative is unable to guess the word, he/she has to construct a sentence before being allowed to return to his/her seat.
4. The representative who guesses the correct answer will win a point for his/her team. Students will take turns to guess and the group with highest score wins.

熱鬧的選舉

Reading

SCENARIO: 以思 and his classmates are very busy this week as the school is filled with activities. What are the special activities in school?

這個星期是以思學校的選舉週。星期一早上，學校裡到處都看得到各種各樣的競選海報。六年級的學生因為年紀比較大也比較有經驗，可以出來競選學生會會長；四年級的學生可以競選學校商店的店員，五年級的學生可以出來競選學校商店裡管錢的工作。參加競選的學生有一個星期的時間進行競選活動，星期五早上每位候選人還要上台演講，讓大家決定要把票投給誰。

以思今年五年級，他決定出來參加競選，因為他覺得自己數學好，可以把管錢的工作做好。這個工作是要把每一分錢都記下來，像學生會原來有多少錢，商店每個月買進來什麼、賣出去什麼，都要算得清清楚楚的。爸爸媽媽都很高興以思做了這個決定，因為這是一個很好的工作經驗，讓他學習怎麼樣管錢。

每一張競選海報都是學生花了很多心思做出來的。有的很簡單，只寫了幾句重要的話；有的畫了很多卡通，讓人覺得很有趣；❶以思是用很多張玩具錢，在海報上排出了自己的名字。

星期五演講那天，每位候選人都很認真地介紹自己。有個很會唱歌的女生，除了唱歌，還找了同學在旁邊跳舞；有個候選人穿得很奇怪，希望大家看了以後就能記住他是誰。以思請了同學和他一起上台演短劇，所有的人看了都大笑起來。

以思跟爸爸說，演講、海報雖然對候選人有幫助，但是最重要的是這個候選人平時是不是很負責，是不是好相處，❷只有大家都相信、都喜歡的人最後才會被選上。

New Words

學生會 xué shēng huì	student council	管 guǎn	manage	會長 huì zhǎng	president
進行 jìn xíng	carry out	上台 shàng tái	go on stage	演講 yǎn jiǎng	give a speech
心思 xīn sī	thought; efforts	畫 huà	draw	演 yǎn	act
短劇 duǎn jù	short play; skit	相信 xiāng xìn	believe		

熱鬧的選舉

Exercises

Check & Resequence

Check the square box if the sentence is depicting the content in the reading passage. Next, number these sentences in the circles according to the sequence in the passage.

☑ ③ Ⓐ 爸媽很高興以思想去學校商店當店員。

☑ ⑥ Ⓑ 以思覺得負(fù)責(zé)、大家都相(xiāng)信(xìn)的人才會當(dāng)選(xuǎn)。

☑ ⑤ Ⓒ 演(yǎn)講(jiǎng)那一天，候(hòu)選(xuǎn)人(rén)用不同的方法讓同學記住自己。

☑ ④ Ⓓ 學校選(xuǎn)舉(jǔ)週到了，不同年級的人可以競(jìng)選(xuǎn)不同的工作。

☒ ○ Ⓔ 以思數學好又很負(fù)責(zé)，所以當(dāng)選(xuǎn)了。

☑ ① Ⓕ 候(hòu)選(xuǎn)人(rén)做了海(hǎi)報(bào)來介紹自己。

☑ ② Ⓖ 以思想要競(jìng)選(xuǎn)學校商店管(guǎn)錢的工作。

☒ ○ Ⓗ 以思不但請同學和他一起唱歌，還一起跳舞。

☐ ○ Ⓘ 爸爸以前也競(jìng)選(xuǎn)過學(xué)生(shēng)會(huì)會(huì)長(zhǎng)。

☒ ○ Ⓙ 以晴也把票(piào)投(tóu)給了以思。

Think & Discuss

Work in pairs and answer the questions in Chinese.

1. 為什麼以思想要競(jìng)選(xuǎn)學校商店管(guǎn)錢的工作？

2. 以思做了哪些事情讓大家記住他？

3. 你參加過競(jìng)選(xuǎn)活動嗎？為了當(dāng)選(xuǎn)，你做了哪些事情？

LESSON 5

Language Focus

1

以思	用	很多張玩具錢，	在	海報上
妹妹		紅筆		白紙上

hǎi bào

| 排出了自己的名字。 |
| 畫出漂亮的花。 |

huà

TIP The word 用 indicates the item to be used while 在 indicates the location. This structure is used to indicate that a particular item is used at a certain location to complete a specific action.

哥哥用綠色的筆在海報上畫出可愛的圖案。
　　　　　　　　　　　hǎi bào　huà　　　　tú àn

我用不同顏色的紙，在門上貼出一朵一朵的小花。

PRACTICE IT Using sentence structure 1, complete the sentences with the helping phrases.

1. 以晴 ___黑筆紅紙上___ 寫吉利話。

2. 弟弟 ___用糖果在盤子上___ 排出數字，要妹妹猜一猜。

3. 媽媽 ___用刀在蛋糕上___ 畫出一條一條的線，
huà
這樣比較容易分給大家吃。

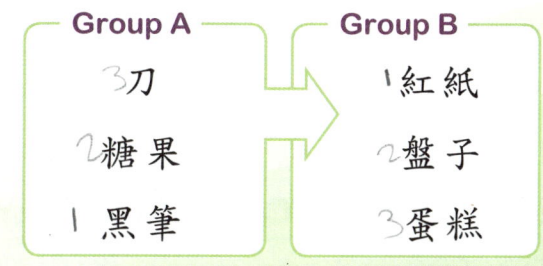

Group A	Group B
3 刀	1 紅紙
2 糖果	2 盤子
1 黑筆	3 蛋糕

熱鬧的選舉

2		大家都相信、都喜歡的人	才	會被選上。
	只有	同學相信你的數學能力，		會把他們的票投給你。

A: 怎麼樣才能當選（dāng xuǎn）？

B: 只有認真又負責（fù zé）的候選人（hòu xuǎn rén），才有機會當選（dāng xuǎn）。

A: 老師，我們可以出去打球了嗎？

B: 只有做完功課的學生，才能出去打球。

TIP: The phrase 只有 is used to indicate the only condition that has to be fulfilled before the target specified after the word 才 can be achieved. The word 才 also indicates that the target is rather difficult to achieve.

Using sentence structure 2, complete the sentences with the helping phrases.

1. A: 你知道爺爺退休後想住在哪裡嗎？
   B: 只有安靜不吵鬧的地方，

2. A: 這次選舉（xuǎn jǔ）要投（tóu）給誰？
   B: 只有看懂了候選人的政見才知。

3. A: 讀歷史真的很簡單（jiǎn dān）嗎？
   B: 對我來說，一點都不簡單（jiǎn dān）。只有花心思弄清楚事件發生的原因

安靜又不吵鬧／候選人（hòu xuǎn rén）的政見（zhèng jiàn）／花心思（xīn sī）弄清楚事件發生的原因

Go700 **WANT TO LEARN MORE?**
Check out the Text > Sentence Pattern section on the Go700 CD-ROM.

熱鬧的選舉

LESSON 5

Listening — Text > Dialogue section

SCENARIO: The results of the student council election have been announced. 以思 breaks the news to everyone the moment he reaches home.

 Listen to the Go700 CD-ROM for the dialogue and answer the following multiple-choice questions.

1. 以思什麼時候開始工作？
   (A) 下個月　(B) 下個星期　(C) 下個星期一

2. 為什麼以思覺得很多人都認得他？
   (A) 他的數學好。　(B) 他的海報(hǎi bào)做得好。
   (C) 他找了很多人談話。

3. 為什麼媽媽覺得同學要選以思？
   (A) 大家都相信(xiāng xìn)他。　(B) 他有很多好朋友。
   (C) 他賣東西賣得比較便宜。

4. 以思下個星期要做什麼？
   (A) 找有經驗的人談談　(B) 到學校商店工作
   (C) 和同學一起做海報(hǎi bào)

5. 下面哪一個句子是對的？
   (A) 爸爸覺得以思能當選(dāng xuǎn)是因為競選海報(jìng xuǎn hǎi bào)做得好。
   (B) 以思要先去弄清楚其他人怎麼做和要注意的事情。
   (C) 大家相信(xiāng xìn)以思會算便宜一點，所以把票投(piào tóu)給他。

New Words

| 能力 néng lì | capabilities | 本來 běn lái | originally |

熱鬧的選舉

B Number the following text in the correct order to form a coherent conversation.

[3] 以思：我想，除了我的數學能力以外，我那張競選海報也幫了我很多忙，____不少忙記____！

[ ] 以思：當然不會！我是管錢的，每樣東西應該賣多少錢，就賣多少錢！我一定會_____！

[1] 以思：爸！我當選了！從下個月開始，我每天都要到學校商店去工作了。

[ ] 媽媽：以思，以後你朋友到商店買東西，你會不會_____？

[ ] 爸爸：最近你應該找時間_____，問問他們有哪些要注意的事情。

[ ] 以思：這我知道，我本來就想下個星期去找他們談談。

[2] 爸爸：管錢是一件重要的工作，一定是你同學____相信你____，才把他們的票投給你。

[ ] 媽媽：我想大家一定是相信你，所以才都把票投給你！

C Listen to the dialogue on the Go700 CD-ROM again, and fill in the blanks.

熱鬧的選舉

LESSON 5

Culture Link

Election Culture

Political elections, be it presidential, provincial, mayoral, etc., have been held in many countries over the years. During the election campaign, many candidates will do their best to let the electorate know them. Besides making their political views known, they will also increase their exposure. Apart from participating in rallies to express their political views and campaign slogan, they will also display their campaign banners along the streets. In places such as Thailand, South Korea, and Hong Kong, candidates will feature their names and election serial numbers on the banners and hang them prominently on wire poles along the streets, hoping that more people will recognize and vote for them. In countries such as Malaysia, supporters of different political parties will hang the flags of respective parties along the streets to show their support. However, in the U.S. and certain European countries, very few candidates will choose to put up campaign banners; the electorate like to attend campaign activities organized by the candidates, listening to their favorite candidates giving a speech as they wave the national flag in support.

What is the election culture in your country? Discuss it with your friends.

the United States

South Korea

Thailand

Malaysia

Hong Kong

熱鬧的選舉

Role Playing

Form groups of four and role-play the scenario. You may use the sentence structures provided below.

CHARACTERS:

爸爸，媽媽，以晴，以思

SCENARIO:
Tomorrow 以思 will start his first day of work at the school store. His parents and 以晴 are talking with him about the work nature and the work attitude that he needs to have.

SENTENCE STRUCTURES:

1. ……用……在……
2. 只有……，才……
3. 要是……，怎麼辦？
4. 對……來說，……
5. 這麼說，……

LESSON 5

Learn about the Chinese Language & Culture

　　選舉(xuǎn jǔ)就跟比賽一樣，一定有輸有贏。選上的人雖然贏了，但是不能因為贏得比賽就很得意。沒選上的人跟輸了比賽的人一樣，要有運動員的*精神(jīng shén)，不到最後一分鐘不*停止(tíng zhǐ)比賽，也不要因為輸了而對自己沒有信心。

　　「*勝(shèng)不*驕(jiāo)，*敗(bài)不*餒(něi)。」你可以把這句話送給所有參加比賽的朋友。不管他們贏了還是輸了，這句話都很有用。

　　在這個句子裡，「勝(shèng)」對「敗(bài)」，「不」對「不」，「驕(jiāo)」對「餒(něi)」。字數一樣、*詞性(cí xìng)相同、句子*組成(zǔ chéng)的*結構(jié gòu)相同，這種句子叫做「*對偶(duì ǒu)」。有些*詞語(cí yǔ)也有對偶(duì ǒu)，像是「鳥語花香」裡的「鳥語」對「花香」，「山高水長」裡的「山高」對「水長」。

　　對偶(duì ǒu)，不只是詞對詞，還有的是長句對長句。

茶，*泡(pào)茶，泡(pào)好茶； 坐，請坐，請上坐。	風聲，雨聲，讀書聲，聲聲入耳； 家事，國事，天下事，事事關心。

GIVE IT A TRY　Work in pairs and come up with a sentence containing an antithesis.

*精神 spirit　　停止 stop　　勝 win　　驕 arrogant　　敗 lose　　餒 disheartened　　詞性 part of speech
組成 form　　結構 structure　　對偶 antithesis　　詞語 word and phrase　　泡 brew

熱鬧的選舉

Work It Out

The school is going to elect a Chinese Language Ambassador and every class will have to send a candidate to contest the election. What are the capabilities and qualities that you think a Chinese Language Ambassador should possess?

TASK
Electing a Chinese Language Ambassador

1. The teacher explains to the class the capabilities and qualities that the Chinese Language Ambassador is expected to possess, as well as the roles and responsibilities that he/she has to undertake.

2. The class is to be divided into groups (depending on the total number of students in class) and each group has to nominate a suitable candidate for the Chinese Language Ambassador; self-nomination is allowed as well.

3. Each group will discuss and come up with the necessary text and content to be featured on campaign banners, and the candidate will have to prepare a speech in Chinese to express his/her views.

4. The students will vote and elect the Chinese Language Ambassador for the class.

LEARNING LOG

I can...

		Excellent	Good	Fair	Need Improvement
1	state the criteria an election candidate has to fulfil, as well as the activities that takes place during the campaign period.	○	○	○	○
2	use "……用……在……" to indicate that a particular item is used at a specific location to complete a certain action.	○	○	○	○
3	use "只有……，才……" to indicate that a condition has to be fulfilled before a specific target can be achieved.	○	○	○	○
4	describe the election culture in some countries.	○	○	○	○
5	tell how an antithesis is used in a sentence and give an example.	○	○	○	○
6	write 投票, 負責, 簡單, and 幫助.	○	○	○	○

LESSON 6

旅行學習
Traveling and Learning

1. What type of tours have you taken?
2. What type of tour do you enjoy? Why?

My Goals

1. Describe the relationship between traveling and learning, and narrate in full one's travel experience
2. Express an action and the duration of the action
3. Describe how certain conditions have to be fulfilled before a target can be met
4. Know how Chinese scripts evolved through the ages
5. Understand the travel taboos in different countries

Get Started

SCENARIO: 安地 is going to take two weeks' leave from school. After class, 以晴 and 久美子 ask him why he is doing so.

A Number the following text in the correct order to form a coherent dialogue.

[2] 安　地：因為爸爸和媽媽要帶我去英國看親人和旅行。

[7] 久美子：今年暑假，媽媽要帶我去小城看退休的爺爺。爺爺喜歡動物，所以我打算送他一隻小貓。以晴呢？

[1] 以　晴：安地，為什麼你要請兩個星期的假？

[6] 安　地：沒問題，我不但會拍照給妳們看，還會買紀念品給妳們。今年暑假，妳們要去哪裡呢？

[8] 以　晴：今年暑假，我哪裡都不去，對我來說，還是在家裡休息最舒服。

[4] 安　地：我之前只有在冬天去英國，我也不知道英國夏天的風景怎麼樣。

[5] 以　晴：那你要把去過的每一個地方都拍下來，像市區、小城、鄉下什麼的。

[3] 久美子：我從來沒去過英國。對我來說，英國是一張一張漂亮的照片。現在是夏天，那裡的風景怎麼樣？

B In groups of three, practice reading out the above conversation. Next, exchange roles and repeat the exercise.

LESSON 6

準備 zhǔnbèi	
xíng lǐ 行李 (luggage)	lǚ xíng xiāng 旅行箱

換 huàn

wài bì
外幣
(foreign currency)

yù dìng
預訂
(reserve)

jī piào 機票 (air ticket)　　lǚ guǎn 旅館 (hotel)

chá
查

dēng jì
登記
(register)

zī liào
資料
(information)

jī wèi
機位
(flight seat)

辦 bàn

qiān zhèng 簽證 (travel visa)　　hù zhào 護照 (passport)

ān pái
安排

bǎo xiǎn 保險 (insurance)　　jià zhào 駕照 (driver's license)

xíng chéng 行程 (itinerary)　　zhù sù 住宿 (accommodation)

zhǔn shí 準時 (on time)　　tí qián 提前 (in advance)

wù diǎn 誤點 (delay; behind schedule (for transportation))　　yán hòu 延後 (postpone)

New Words

| chá 查 | check | ān pái 安排 | arrange | lǚ xíng xiāng 旅行箱 | travel suitcase |

Black Matches White

1. The teacher makes word cards of the above new words; nouns are written on white cards, verbs on black cards, and "準時, 誤點, 提前, 延後" on red cards.
2. The teacher keeps the red cards and distributes the remaining cards randomly to all students. When the teacher reads out a verb, the student with the corresponding verb card and the student with a noun card that can be used with the verb have to stand up. If they fail to do so, they have to construct sentences with the verb and noun.
3. If the teacher reads out words of any red cards, all students have to stand up and the last to do so or those who fail to stand up have to construct sentences with the word they are holding.
4. The student with the least number of fouls wins the game.

旅行學習

Reading

SCENARIO: 以晴 and her family are going overseas for a holiday. Where are they going? When are they leaving? What are the preparations that they need to make before setting off?

今年四月，爸爸要到日本❶開三天的會，爸爸決定帶大家一起去看看這個東方國家。他們有兩星期的假，可以去三個城市旅行，大家都很興奮。

久美子的媽媽告訴他們，日本是一個不太喜歡說英文的國家，❷他們需要做好出發前的準備，才會有快樂的旅行。因為家裡沒有人會說日文，爸爸要大家上網，找到英文和日文的旅行會話，把重要的、可能用到的句子都整理出來、印出來，大家一起練習。媽媽也請久美子一家到家裡吃飯，請他們介紹日本，還有去日本旅行應該注意的地方。

除了練習日文會話，媽媽還把工作列在一張單子上，要大家開始準備。每個人的工作是：

1. 爸爸負責安排交通和住的地方。
2. 媽媽除了管錢以外，還要負責跟白爺爺聯絡，請他幫忙看家和照顧小狗雪球。
3. 以晴要準備一張單子，把旅行要帶的東西列出來。

旅行學習

4. 以安要負責把旅行要帶的東西整理好，放進旅行箱。

5. 以思要上網查日本這三個城市的天氣，告訴大家要穿什麼樣的衣服。

另外，以安、以晴和以思，每個人要負責一個城市，列出要參觀的地方、怎麼去、有什麼好玩的、要花多少時間、要花多少錢，還要把參觀地點在地圖上畫出來。開會時，大家再投票決定去哪裡玩。

媽媽說：「旅行好像讀書，除了課本上的知識外，還得多到各地旅行，讓自己知道得更多。每一次的旅行都是很好的經驗，都是很好的學習機會。」她希望大家從日本旅行回來以後，都對這個東方國家有更多的認識。

New Words

上網 go on the Internet	開會 have a meeting	東方 East; Oriental	出發 set out; depart
會話 conversation	印 print	列 list	聯絡 contact
另外 in addition	花 spend	地點 site; location	知識 knowledge

Exercises

True or False?

Answer the questions according to the reading passage.　　　　　　　　對　錯

1. 因為工作的關係,爸爸要去日本。　○　○
2. 以晴他們得把日文學好,才能去旅行。　○　○
3. 除了爸爸,每個人都有自己要準備的工作。　○　○
4. 媽媽需要請白爺爺教她怎麼管錢,因為這是她要準備的工作。　○　○
5. 以安、以晴和以思要找出在日本可以去哪裡玩。　○　○
6. 要學習課本上的知zhī識shì,得多到世界各地旅行。　○　○

Think & Discuss

Work in pairs and answer the questions in Chinese.

1. 以晴一家人為了旅行要做什麼準備?
2. 為什麼媽媽說旅行就像讀書一樣?
3. 你跟家人一起去旅行過嗎?旅行前,你們做了哪些準備工作?

LESSON 6

Travel Taboos

There are many languages, cultures, and ethnic groups across the world. Before traveling, other than planning itineraries and checking on transportation and accommodation, it is also necessary to understand the culture and taboos of the destination country. This would ensure a smoother and safer trip.

Here are a few examples:

❶ Cows are considered sacred in India, and travelers should refrain from wearing anything made from cows when entering a Hindu temple.

❷ In Myanmar and Cambodia, it is considered impolite to touch someone's head and hence travelers should refrain from touching the heads of the children there.

❸ As the Japanese are very particular about punctuality, travelers should be punctual for appointments in Japan.

❹ The people in the Middle East are predominantly Muslims who consider the left hand to be unclean, so travelers should use their right hand when shaking hands or eating.

❺ In Denmark, drinking and toasting is a social norm and when "Skal" is said while toasting, one will have to bottoms up and finish the drink.

❻ When traveling in America, conversations on race should be avoided.

❼ In places where Chinese are predominant, such as Taiwan, Hong Kong, and China, there are etiquette rules for the use of chopsticks: chopsticks should <u>not</u> be inserted vertically in a bowl of rice, or be used to point at people.

In order to understand local customs, travelers should carefully read the related information before they set out. Traveling does not involve just the traveler as local customs and people are also part of the picture. Therefore, travelers should respect the culture of their destination country and try to "do as the Romans do when in Rome". This reduces travel inconveniences, and locals will likely appreciate it and reciprocate by extending their warmth and hospitality.

Are there any special travel taboos in your country? Discuss them with your classmates.

Language Focus

1

| 開（了） | 三天 | 會 |
| 放（了） | 兩星期 | 的 假 |

kāi / huì

A: 你昨天讀多久的書？
B: 我昨天讀了兩個多小時的書。

A: 從商場走路到學校很遠嗎？
B: 從商場到學校要走二十分鐘的路。

TIP This structure indicates an action and the duration of the action. When using the structure, note that the form can be "Verb + Noun" such as 開會, or "Verb + Verb" like 練習. For the former, the words that denote the duration are inserted between the verb and the noun, such as 開(了)三天的會; for the latter, the words denoting the duration are placed after the verb, such as 練習三十分鐘. Also, when describing a completed action, the word 了 should be inserted after the verb, such as 開了三天的會.

PRACTICE IT

Using sentence structure 1, complete the dialogue with the helping phrases.

1. A: 你知道從日本搭飛機到歐洲要花多久時間嗎？
   B: 從日本搭飛機到歐洲要花十幾個小時

2. A: 火車又誤點了嗎？
   B: 是啊！____兩個小時____，火車還是沒來。

3. A: 為什麼媽媽很擔心小明？
   B: 因為他很早就出發了，可是給他____打電話_____一個小時_____，他都沒有接。

Group A	Group B
一個小時	坐飛機
兩個小時	吃飯
十幾個小時	打電話

LESSON 6

2	他們	需要	做好出發前的準備， (chū fā)	才	會有快樂的旅行。
	我們		多吃青菜和水果，		會有健康的身體。

A: 弟弟能做好這件事嗎？
B: 他**需要**你的幫忙，**才**能做好這件事。

TIP This sentence structure indicates that the condition stated after the phrase 需要 has to be satisfied before the target specified after the word 才 can be achieved.

A: 我要怎麼做才能當選？
B: 你**需要**做好競選的準備工作，但是最重要的是做事要負責，大家**才**會把票投給你。

 **PRACTICE IT**

Using sentence structure 2, complete the dialogue with the helping phrases.

1. A: 你覺得怎麼樣的候選人才會當選？
   B: 候選人需要認真負責才能當選 （認真負責）

2. A: 你安排住宿的時候需要上網嗎？ (ān pái zhù sù) (shàng wǎng)
   B: 我需要上網，才可以預訂住宿 （預訂住宿）(yù dìng zhù sù)

3. A: 出國之前要準備哪些資料？ (zī liào)
   B: _____ （辦護照）(hù zhào)

Check out the Text > Sentence Pattern section on the Go700 CD-ROM.

旅行學習

Listening

Text > Dialogue section

SCENARIO: 以晴 just returned from her holiday in Japan. 久美子 sees 以晴 in school and greets her happily. The girls start talking about the trip.

A Listen to the Go700 CD-ROM for the dialogue and answer the following multiple-choice questions.

1. 以晴在Kyoto看到了什麼？
   (A) 高樓大廈（dà xià） (B) 古老（gǔ lǎo）的房子 (C) 美麗的海

2. 久美子明年暑假可能去哪裡？
   (A) Tokyo   (B) Kyoto   (C) Yokohama

3. 要是久美子去旅行，她希望以晴幫她什麼？
   (A) 教她一些中文。
   (B) 給她介紹好吃的食物。
   (C) 給她介紹好玩的城市。

4. 星期六下午以晴跟久美子要做什麼？
   (A) 買點心 (B) 看照片 (C) 整理照片

5. 下面哪一個句子是對的？
   (A) 久美子明年暑假要和以晴一起去旅行。
   (B) 久美子介紹很多日本的點心給以晴。
   (C) 久美子星期六下午要去以晴家。

New Words

| 大廈 (dà xià) | building | 古老 (gǔ lǎo) | ancient |

B Number the following text in the correct order to form a coherent conversation.

[ ] 久美子：別客氣！下次我到＿＿＿＿＿＿的時候，也請妳教我幾句＿＿＿＿＿＿。

[1] 久美子：以晴，妳回來了！妳覺得日本好玩嗎？你們去了哪些城市？

[ ] 以　晴：好啊！我還從日本帶回來＿＿＿＿＿＿，到時候一起吃！

[ ] 久美子：我沒去過Yokohama，希望明年暑假的時候，我＿＿＿＿＿＿＿＿＿＿。

[ ] 以　晴：當然沒問題！對了，旅行的時候，我們拍了很多照片，這個＿＿＿＿＿＿＿＿＿，妳想不想來我家看照片？

[ ] 久美子：好啊！我也回去整理一些在日本拍的照片，帶到妳家一起看。

[ ] 以　晴：妳教我們的那幾句日文，真是太有用了！謝謝妳！

[ ] 以　晴：我們去了Tokyo、Kyoto和Yokohama。在Tokyo看到了很多＿＿＿＿＿＿高樓大廈(dà xià)；在Kyoto看到了很多古(gǔ)老(lǎo)的＿＿＿＿＿＿；在Yokohama看到了＿＿＿＿＿＿。

C Listen to the dialogue on the Go700 CD-ROM again, and fill in the blanks.

旅行學習

xíng wàn lǐ lù shèng dú wàn juàn shū
「行萬里路勝讀萬卷書」

Traveling Ten Thousand Miles Beats Reading Ten Thousand Books

People of the past already knew that reading alone is insufficient, and that they should travel to broaden their horizons. The saying "行萬里路勝讀萬卷書" aptly describes this. However, as transportation was not well developed in the past, to literally "行萬里路" (travel ten thousand miles) could be a challenging yet special experience; and for most people, it could only remain a dream.

Today, with the advancement in transportation, most of the places around the world can be reached within a single day. Now "行萬里路" is no longer a distant dream and has even become part of daily life for some people. Therefore, we should make full use of every opportunity to travel. Through traveling, not only can we see for ourselves the knowledge acquired from books, we can also enrich our own lives by experiencing the cultures and lifestyle of different places.

 In your native language, do you have any phrases or idioms that mean "行萬里路勝讀萬卷書"? Share with your fellow classmates.

Form groups of four and role-play the scenario. You may use the sentence structures provided below.

CHARACTERS:

久美子, 以晴, 以安, 以思

SCENARIO:
以晴 and family just came back from their holiday in Japan and 久美子 visits 以晴 to see their travel photos. While viewing the photos, 以晴 and her siblings also talk about how they prepared for the trip and what happened during the trip.

SENTENCE STRUCTURES:

1. Verb (了) + Time + Noun
2. ……需要……，才……
3. ……用……在……
4. 要是……，怎麼辦？
5. 對……來說，……
6. 這麼說，……

LESSON 6

Learn about the Chinese Language & Culture

　　*漢字在不同的*時代有不同的*流行*字體。漢字字體的*變化，可以分為五種：*篆書(大篆、小篆)、*隸書、*草書、*楷書、*行書。從下面的圖片，你可以看到在不同的時代被*刻在*石頭上的字。

篆書

周－秦 (Zhou-Qin Dynasty, B.C. 1046 - B.C. 206)

隸書

秦－漢 (Qin-Han Dynasty, B.C. 221 – A.D. 220)

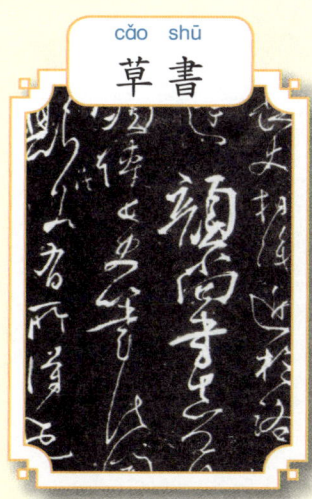

草書

漢－唐 (Han-Tang Dynasty, B.C. 206 - A.D. 907)

楷書

漢－現在 (Han Dynasty - now, B.C. 206 - now)

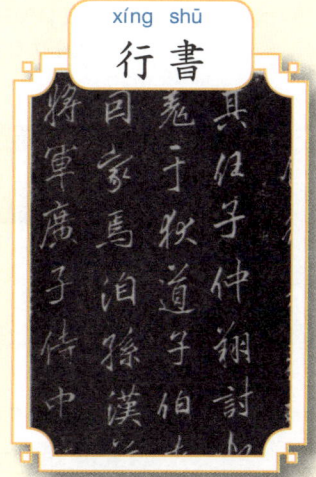

行書

晉 (Jin Dynasty, A.D. 265 - A.D. 420)

*漢字 Chinese characters　　時代 era　　流行 popular　　字體 typeface; style of script　　變化 change
篆書 seal script (大篆 large seal script、小篆 small seal script)　　隸書 official script　　行書 running/semi-cursive script
草書 cursive script　　楷書 regular script　　刻 carve; engrave　　石頭 stone

Work It Out

The most important aspect of a holiday trip is the preparation work. There are itineraries to plan, accommodation to check, and budget to control. Have you ever organized a holiday trip?

TASK

Organizing a Holiday Trip

1. The teacher instructs students to cut out the holiday planning form on page 161.
2. Each student is to write down a preferred holiday destination on a piece of paper and drop it into a box.
3. Divide the class into groups of four to five. Each group sends a representative to the teacher to draw a holiday destination.
4. The representative will then throw the dice to determine the number of days and the budget for their holiday trip. Each group will have to plan their trip accordingly. They will also discuss what souvenirs to buy and for whom, and subsequently complete the form.
5. When the planning is done, each group is to send a representative to present the itinerary.
6. After the presentation, the class will vote for the best travel itinerary.

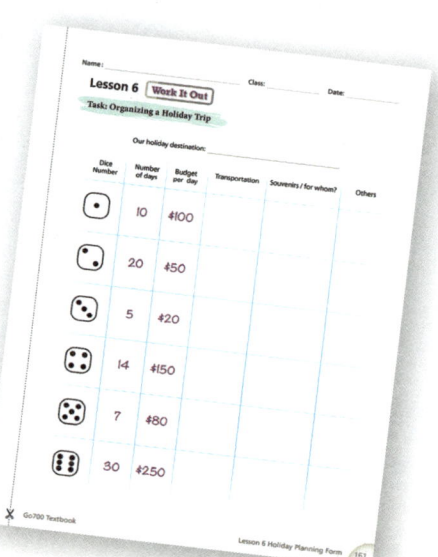

LEARNING LOG

I can...   Excellent | Good | Fair | Need Improvement

1. narrate one holiday trip in full, and talk about the relationship between traveling and learning.
2. use " Verb (了) + Time + Noun" to indicate an action and the duration of that action.
3. use "……需要……，才……" to express the situation in which a target can only be met when certain conditions have been fulfilled.
4. understand how Chinese scripts evolved through the ages.
5. give examples of travel taboos in different countries.
6. write 上網, 開會, 另外, and 聯絡.

86　旅行學習

LESSON 7

爸爸失業了
Dad Is Out of Work

1. How does this man look like?
2. What do you think has happened to him?

My Goals

1. Understand the importance of increasing income and reducing expenditure
2. Describe the methods required to resolve a certain problem
3. Express that one does not have an opinion, interest, or notion regarding a particular subject
4. Understand the wage system in different countries
5. Recognize and understand Chinese metaphors

SCENARIO: 以晴 follows her mother to do grocery shopping and passes by a job agency. Through the window, she sees a lot of people, some waiting in a queue, and others filling up application forms.

A Complete the conversation by using the sentence structures provided and the hints in parentheses.

```
A. 有的……，有的……
B. 需要……，才……
C. 除了……，還……
D. Verb（了）+ Time + Noun
```

以晴：沒想到現在那麼多人沒有工作。

媽媽：對，_____（找工作/換工作）

以晴：到這裡，就一定找得到工作嗎？

媽媽：不一定，_____（半年/找工作），還是找不到。

以晴：他們的運氣真不好。

媽媽：現在找工作，_____

_____（運氣/工作能力）

以晴：所以我現在_____（認真讀書）

媽媽：以晴這麼聰明，我相信妳以後一定可以找到一份好工作。

B In pairs, practice reading out the above conversation. Next, exchange roles and repeat the exercise.

LESSON 7

Vocabulary Builder

JOBS

gōng sī	kāi chú
公司	開除 (sack; dismiss)

cái yuán	zhí yè
裁員 (retrench; lay off)	職業 (career; job)

zhèng zhí	jiān zhí
正職 (full-time job)	兼職 (part-time work)

cún qián	xīn shuǐ
存錢 (save money)	薪水 (salary; wage)

shí xīn	yuè xīn
時薪 (hourly pay)	月薪 (monthly pay)

nián xīn	xué fèi
年薪 (annual income)	學費 (school fees)

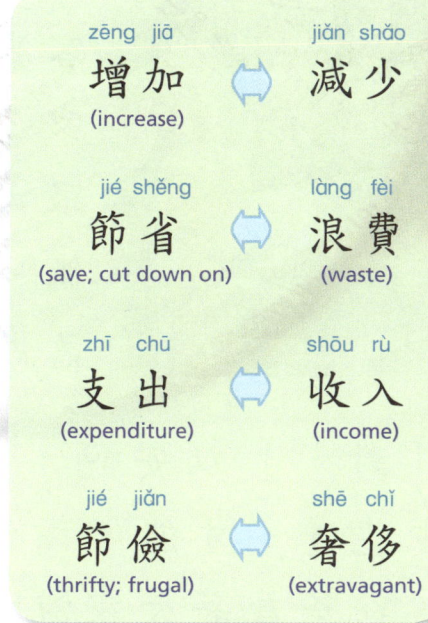

zēng jiā	jiǎn shǎo
增加 (increase)	減少

jié shěng	làng fèi
節省 (save; cut down on)	浪費 (waste)

zhī chū	shōu rù
支出 (expenditure)	收入 (income)

jié jiǎn	shē chǐ
節儉 (thrifty; frugal)	奢侈 (extravagant)

kāi yuán jié liú	kè qín kè jiǎn	huī jīn rú tǔ
開源節流 (increase income and reduce expenditure)	克勤克儉 (be diligent and frugal)	揮金如土 (squander; spend money without restraint)

New Words

jiǎn shǎo		gōng sī	
減少	reduce; cut down	公司	company

Fun with Fishing

1. Teacher prepares a set of word cards with magnets affixed on their back, a container, and a pole with a magnet attached to it.
2. Divide the class into two groups. Each group will receive a piece of paper with nine squares drawn on it, and students can choose any of the nine new words, and write down their *pinyin* in the squares.
3. Students from the two groups take turns to "fish" for their word cards. If the word card they fish corresponds to a *pinyin* word in one of the squares, they can paste the word card on that square.
4. The first team to fill up all nine squares with word cards wins the game.

爸爸失業了

Reading

SCENARIO: Something is about to happen to Sunny's family today. After dinner, Sunny's father announces the news to the family.

吃完晚飯，爸爸要大家在客廳坐下。他有一件事要告訴大家。爸爸說：「吃飯時，我常常跟大家談工作的情形，我想，你們一定注意到爸爸的公司最近生意做得不太好。」

「對，」以安說：「好像❶你們公司不太賺錢，得減少花費，才能繼續做下去。」「是的，以安說對了！」爸爸看著大家說：「減少花費就是得減少工作人員，爸爸從明天開始就沒有工作了，不用去上班了。」

「什麼？爸爸，你是說你失業了？」以晴大叫：「我們以後怎麼辦呢？」爸爸說：「我在公司做了十多年，公司會給我一些錢，政府也會給我半年的失業金，讓我安心找工作。」

「如果半年以後，爸爸還是找不到工作呢？」以晴小心地問。「我想應該不會，」爸爸說：「但是，我們得做最壞的打算，所以，從今天起，我們的生活會有些不同。」

爸爸失業了

以安說：「我下課以後，可以去打工。」以晴說：「我可以不買午餐，自己帶三明治去學校，我也可以不要零用錢。」以思說：「我可以不學中國功夫，我也可以每星期少拿一點兒零用錢。」

爸爸笑了，他說：「謝謝你們！你們願意跟爸爸媽媽一起減少花費，爸爸很高興。爸爸會努力去找工作，只是在找到工作以前，我們不能去旅行，也不能每星期去餐廳吃飯了。」「沒問題，」以思跑去抱住爸爸，說：「爸爸沒有了工作，可是爸爸還有我們，我們不會賺錢，但是我們會少花錢。」

New Words

情形 qíng xíng — circumstance; situation	花費 huā fèi — expense; expenditure	繼續 jì xù — continue
人員 rén yuán — staff; personnel	失業 shī yè — out of work	政府 zhèng fǔ — government
失業金 shī yè jīn — unemployment compensation	打算 dǎ suàn — plan	抱住 bào zhù — hug

Exercises

Complete the Chart

Complete the chart based on the reading passage.

地點：＿＿＿＿＿＿＿＿＿＿＿＿＿＿＿＿＿＿＿＿＿＿＿＿＿＿＿

參加的人：＿＿＿＿＿＿＿＿＿＿＿＿＿＿＿＿＿＿＿＿＿＿＿

事情：＿＿＿＿＿＿＿＿＿＿＿＿＿＿＿＿＿＿＿＿＿＿＿＿＿＿
＿＿＿＿＿＿＿＿＿＿＿＿＿＿＿＿＿＿＿＿＿＿＿＿＿＿＿＿＿

以安、以晴和以思會怎麼做？

以安：＿＿＿＿＿＿＿＿＿＿＿＿＿＿＿＿＿＿＿＿＿＿＿＿＿

以晴：＿＿＿＿＿＿＿＿＿＿＿＿＿＿＿＿＿＿＿＿＿＿＿＿＿

以思：＿＿＿＿＿＿＿＿＿＿＿＿＿＿＿＿＿＿＿＿＿＿＿＿＿

Think & Discuss

Work in pairs and answer the questions in Chinese.

1. 為什麼以晴一家人不能去旅行了？

2. 公司和政府會怎麼幫助以晴的爸爸？
   (gōng sī) (zhèng fǔ)

3. 如果你的爸爸或媽媽失業了，你覺得你的生活會有什麼不同？你可以怎麼做？
   (shī yè)

LESSON 7

Culture Link

kāi yuán jié liú
「開源節流」
Increasing Revenue Sources and Reducing Expenditure

"開源節流" is a common Chinese virtue when it comes to money. 開源 refers to developing new sources of income and revenue, while 節流 refers to cutting down on spending. However, it can be rather difficult to establish new sources of income on top of one's existing employment. Hence, a relatively more practical method to accumulate wealth is to review one's lifestyle and cut down on personal expenditure. This is why the Chinese generally manage their expenses on a "need-to-spend" basis to avoid squandering money away, and their frugal spending habits also helped them save up money for other future plans or emergency use. For that reason, thriftiness has become a common trait in many Chinese people, who prefer saving up their money and assets, rather than spending them on short-term indulgences.

TALK ABOUT IT

Is there a similar concept towards money in your country? Do you like this concept? Why?

爸爸失業了

1

你們公司不太賺錢，	得	減少花費。(jiǎn shǎo huā fèi)
爸爸的公司不賺錢，(gōng sī)		減少工作人員。(jiǎn shǎo rén yuán)

A: 你不跟我們一起去看電影嗎？
B: 我明天要考試，得回家看書。

A: 你知道要怎麼存錢嗎？(cún qián)
B: 想要存錢，你得先節省支出。(cún qián) (jié shěng zhī chū)

> **TIP**
> This sentence structure used to describe methods required to resolve certain problems. Here, the word 得 should be pronounced as "děi", and it means "must, have to". The word 得 is preceded by a difficult situation, and the solution is stated after 得.

 Using sentence structure 1, complete the dialogues with the helping phrases.

1. A: 聽說你打算去日本工作，要做什麼準備呢？(dǎ suàn)
   B: <u>去日本工作以前,我得先學好日文</u> （學好日文）

2. A: 有什麼辦法可以增加收入？(zēng jiā shōu rù)
   B: <u>你想增加收入,除了得繼續工作還得兼職。</u> （繼續工作/兼職）(jì xù / jiān zhí)

3. A: 要怎麼做才可以得到這份工作？
   B: 如果<u>想得到這份工作,你得去學中文,增加語言能力。</u> （學中文/增加語言能力）(zēng jiā)

Listening

SCENARIO: After class, 以晴, 久美子, 安地, and 阿明 are chatting at the school café. They talk about the job they would like to do in the future.

A Listen to the Go700 CD-ROM for the dialogue and answer the following multiple-choice questions.

1. 久美子以後想要做什麼？
   - (A) 在家照顧孩子
   - (B) 電腦工程師
   - (C) 到公司(gōng sī)上班

2. 以晴對什麼工作沒興趣？
   - (A) 照顧孩子 (B) 作家 (C) 電腦工程師

3. 以晴以前想要做什麼？
   - (A) 當醫生 (B) 在公司(gōng sī)上班 (C) 到全世界去旅行

4. 久美子覺得大家現在應該做什麼？
   - (A) 一直去打工 (B) 多學習 (C) 常常旅行

5. 下面哪一個句子是對的？
   - (A) 安地想要當在公司(gōng sī)上班的電腦工程師。
   - (B) 阿明對電腦工程師很有興趣。
   - (C) 安地對語言一點兒興趣都沒有。

爸爸失業了

B Number the following text in the correct order to form a coherent conversation.

[1] 以　晴：你們有沒有想過以後要做什麼呢？

[8] 久美子：不管以後做什麼，現在都應該 <u>多學一點兒不同的東西</u>。懂的東西越多越好！

[2] 久美子：以後我想跟媽媽一樣，在家裡 <u>照顧孩子</u>。

[6] 安　地：我現在在學 <u>中文和西班牙文</u>，因為以後我想到 <u>全世界去旅行</u>。以晴，妳呢？

[4] 以　晴：雖然電腦很重要，可是❷我對電腦一點兒興趣都沒有，以後還要請你多幫忙！

[5] 阿　明：不用等到以後，現在我也幫妳 <u>處理電腦問題啊</u>！安地，你以後想做什麼？

[7] 以　晴：以前我想當醫生，現在我覺得能在 <u>公司上班</u> 也不錯。

[3] 阿　明：我喜歡跟電腦有關的工作，我想當個 <u>電腦工程師</u>。

C Listen to the dialogue on the Go700 CD-ROM again, and fill in the blanks.

爸爸失業了

LESSON 7

2	我	對	電腦	一點兒	興趣	都沒有。
	弟弟		_{kāi yuán jié liú} 開源節流		看法	

A: 你以後想做什麼？
B: 我**對**以後的職業_{zhí yè}**一點兒**想法**都沒有**。

A: 今年暑假我們一起去打工吧！
B: 我想找正職_{zhèng zhí}的工作；我**對**打工**一點兒**興趣**都沒有**。

TIP The structure "……對……一點兒……都沒有" expresses in a tactful way that one does not have an opinion, interest, or notion regarding a certain topic.

 Rewrite the sentences using sentence structure 2.

1. 哥哥對這次的候選人都沒有看法。
   ~~哥哥對這次的候選人~~一點兒有看法都沒有

2. 妹妹對這個歷史事件沒有想法。
   妹妹對這個歷史事件一點兒想法都沒有

3. 我對做點心沒興趣。
   我對做點心一點兒都沒有

Check out the Text > Sentence Pattern section on the Go700 CD-ROM.

Wage System

Different countries adopt different wage system. In the East, countries such as China, Japan, Singapore, and the Philippines mainly adopt a monthly pay system. On the other hand, the wage system in the West varies by company and there are companies that pay out salaries twice a month (mid-month and end-of-month), thereby increasing the propensity to spend. Compared to the West, people in the East have higher saving rates and their propensity to spend is relatively lower. Conversely, in the West, many parents encourage their children to be independent as they reach adulthood, and hence a lot of students do part-time work. However, parents in the East would prefer their children to focus on academic studies.

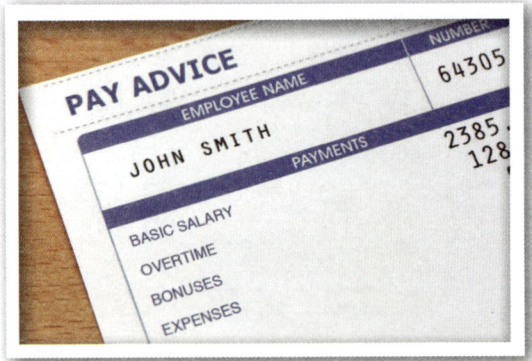

 Do most companies in your country adopt a monthly pay system or weekly pay system? If you are working now, do you prefer receiving your pay weekly or monthly?

Form groups of four and role-play the scenario. You may use the sentence structures provided below.

CHARACTERS:

久美子, 以安, 以晴, 以思

SCENARIO:
When 久美子 visits 以晴, 以晴 and her siblings tell her that their father had lost his job. They talk about some of the changes that may happen in the future, and how they will cope with it.

SENTENCE STRUCTURES:

1. ……，得……
2. ……對……一點兒……都沒有
3. Verb（了）+ Time + Noun
4. ……需要……，才……
5. 要是……，怎麼辦？
6. 對……來說，……

LESSON 7

Learn about the Chinese Language & Culture

　　有些詞很有趣，像是「飯碗」，除了指「吃飯的 *用具(yòng jù)」以外，還可以 *代表(dài biǎo)「工作」。在這一課中，以晴的爸爸沒了工作，我們可以說「以晴的爸爸丟了飯碗」，我們用「丟飯碗」來 *形容(xíng róng)失去工作。

　　這裡還有幾個跟飯碗有關的詞：

找飯碗：找工作

金飯碗：*安定(ān dìng)而且 *收入(shōu rù)很高的工作

*鐵(tiě)飯碗：*穩定(wěn dìng)的或 *國家機關(guó jiā jī guān)的工作

*搶(qiǎng)飯碗：一份工作有很多人要做

*砸(zá)飯碗：因為自己做了不好的事，而讓自己失去工作

*泥(ní)飯碗：不 *穩定(wěn dìng)的工作

　　在生活中，我們常常用 *比喻詞(bǐ yù cí)來代表一件事，你知道下面這些 *比喻詞(bǐ yù cí)是什麼意思嗎？

1 *拍馬屁(pāi mǎ pì)

2 *紙老虎(zhǐ lǎo hǔ)

3 *炒魷魚(chǎo yóu yú)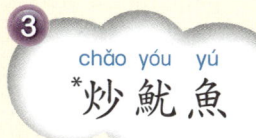

*用具 tool　　代表 represent　　形容 describe　　安定 stable　　收入 income　　鐵 iron　　穩定 stable
國家機關 government agency　　搶 snatch　　砸 smash　　泥 mud　　比喻詞 metaphor
拍馬屁 (lit.) pat a horse's ass　　紙老虎 (lit.) paper tiger　　炒魷魚 (lit.) stir-fry cuttlefish

Work It Out

Everyone will encounter unhappy events in their lives. What would you do when you encounter such events? If your friends encounter events that upset them, how do you go about helping them?

TASK

Sharing on Unhappy Events

1. In groups of three or four, the students share the following:
   (1) What are some unhappy events you have encountered? What are your thoughts after they happened?
   (2) If your friends encounter similar circumstances, what kind of advice or help would you offer?

2. Within each group, students note down the different problems faced and suggestions provided.

3. Each group is to send a representative to share with the class the issues that he or she faced and the suggestions provided by the team.

4. After each presentation, allow 5-10 minutes for students in other groups to provide solutions or suggestions.

LEARNING LOG

I can...

	Excellent	Good	Fair	Need Improvement
1 tell the importance of increasing income and reducing expenditure, and suggest a few methods to achieve this goal.	○	○	○	○
2 use "⋯⋯，得⋯⋯" to state the steps that have to be taken in order to resolve a certain issue.	○	○	○	○
3 use "⋯⋯對⋯⋯一點兒⋯⋯都沒有" to express that one has no opinion, interest, or notion regarding a certain subject.	○	○	○	○
4 understand the wage system in different countries.	○	○	○	○
5 come up with two examples of Chinese metaphors.	○	○	○	○
6 write 政府, 失業, 減少, and 花費.	○	○	○	○

爸爸失業了

LESSON 8

精彩的奧運
The Exciting Olympics

1. Do you know what they are doing?
2. Do you prefer to watch team or individual sports competitions? Why?

My Goals

1. Understand the meaning of sportsmanship and team spirit
2. Explain the cause and effect of a circumstance
3. Indicate a particular situation in which certain essential conditions must be fulfilled
4. Evaluate a topic stated earlier
5. Understand that the word 不 can be used to reinforce an affirmative expression
6. Know the origins of the Olympic Games

SCENARIO: 阿明 wants to join a new extra-curriculum activity this term. He seeks the opinions of 以安 and 久美子.

A Look at the pictures and complete the conversation by using the sentence structures provided.

阿　　明：我想參加*籃球隊，你們覺得打籃球怎麼樣？

久美子：別問我，我<u>對打籃球一點兒興趣都沒有</u>。（……對……一點兒……都沒有）

以　　安：打籃球是很好的運動。<u>除了對身體好，還很有意思</u>。（除了……，還……）

阿　　明：我沒打過籃球，我怕我打得不好。

久美子：打籃球的人<u>不是長得越高越好嗎</u>？（越……越……）你長得高，一定會打得很好，我對你有信心。

阿　　明：大家都說<u>籃球要打得好，得跑得很快</u>（……，得……），但是我跑得很慢。

以　　安：別擔心，我們一起練習，你一定會越跑越快的。

*籃球 basketball

B In groups of three, practice reading out the above conversation. Next, exchange roles and repeat the exercise.

LESSON 8

Vocabulary Builder

ào yùn	lán qiú	tǐ cāo	tiào shuǐ	bǎi mǐ jiē lì sài
奧運	籃球	體操	跳水	百米接力賽

xuǎn shǒu	guó jiā dài biǎo	cái pàn	fàn guī	gōng píng
選手	國家代表	裁判	犯規	公平
	(national representative)	(referee; umpire)	(foul)	(fair)

míng cì	guàn jūn	yà jūn	jì jūn	jiǎng bēi
名次	冠軍	亞軍	季軍	獎盃
(ranking)	(champion)	(runner-up)	(second runner-up)	(trophy)

jiǎng pái	pò jì lù	jiāo ào	qì něi	gǔ lì
獎牌	破紀錄	驕傲	氣餒	鼓勵
(medal)	(record-breaking)	(proud)	(feel discouraged)	(encourage)

New Words

ào yùn 奧運 | Olympic Games	lán qiú 籃球 | basketball	tǐ cāo 體操 | gymnastics	tiào shuǐ 跳水 | diving
bǎi mǐ 百米 | 100 meters	jiē lì sài 接力賽 | relay race	xuǎn shǒu 選手 | athlete; contestant	

Guess Who I Am

1. Students form groups of five, and the teacher prepares a set of word cards and a timer. Students in each group are to decide their order to play.
2. Group A students stand in a line facing the wall, and students in the other groups paste a word card behind Group A's students, who are not supposed to turn around until it is their turn to start the game.
3. The teacher shouts out "猜猜我是誰" and starts to time the game. Then, the first two students in Group A are to step out, and Student 1 will have to guess the word card behind him/her based on clues given by Student 2. If the word is mentioned while giving the clues, the teacher will change the word card immediately for Student 1 to guess again.
4. After each team has completed their round of guessing, the teacher compares each group's timing and the team with the fastest timing wins.

精彩的奧運

Reading

SCENARIO: The Olympics Games are here again. One afternoon, 以晴 and her family are in the living room watching the live telecast and talking about the matches.

四年一次的奧運又到了，以晴一家人都坐在電視機前看奧運。有一個選手摔倒了兩次，雖然腳受傷了，可是還是很努力地跑，以晴覺得他很可憐，一直對著他叫「加油」。以思問媽媽：「這個人已經不可能拿前三名了，為什麼還要繼續跑呢？」

媽媽說：「選手參加比賽，最重要的是運動精神，得獎當然好，得不到獎也沒關係。雖然這個選手沒機會拿到前三名，可是他還是繼續跑到最後，把應該做的事做完。這就是運動精神，大家都會為他加油。」

接下來是四百公尺接力賽。以晴問：「一個選手跑一百公尺，哪個國家的選手多，哪個國家的選手跑得快就會贏，不是嗎？」爸爸搖搖頭，說：「不是。① 接力賽不只要跑得快，接棒子的時候還要接得好，因此選手們還是需要練習很多次。」

該籃球上場了。「投啊！投啊！」以思一直幫美國隊加油：「奇怪！這個人拿到球怎麼不投呢？」以安說：「他是隊長啊！雖然他自己投得進，可是，他要給其他球員得分的機會。如果每次都是隊長投，他的球員就不會跟他配合，對手也只要看著他就好了。這樣，他的隊就不容易得分。所以 ❷ 打籃球的時候，所有的球員一定要一起合作才行。」

媽媽問：「奧運有這麼多比賽，你們最喜歡什麼？」以安說：「我喜歡看籃球比賽，它是團隊運動，需要大家合作，打起來很精彩。」以晴說：「我最喜歡看體操，體操選手的動作真是美極了！可是，看的時候也很緊張，我真怕他們會摔下來。」以思說：「還是跳水最好玩，跳下來就比完了，贏就贏，輸就輸，不會緊張太久。」

New Words

加油 jiā yóu — cheer someone on	運動精神 yùn dòng jīng shén — sportsmanship	公尺 gōng chǐ — meter	接 jiē — receive (something)
棒子 bàng zi — baton	因此 yīn cǐ — therefore; hence	投／投籃 tóu／tóu lán — shoot a ball through the basket	
隊長 duì zhǎng — team captain	球員 qiú yuán — ballgame player	得分 dé fēn — score	配合 pèi hé — coordinate
對手 duì shǒu — opponent	看 kān — guard; keep an eye on	團隊 tuán duì — team	動作 dòng zuò — action

精彩的奧運

Exercises

True or False?

Answer the questions according to the reading passage.   對　錯

1. 運動精神就是不管輸贏，都要比賽到最後。 ✓ ○
2. 接力賽只要選手接棒子接得好就會贏得比賽。 ○ ✓
3. 籃球隊長因為自己打得不好，所以要其他球員跟他配合。 ○ ✓
4. 以安喜歡看需要合作的運動比賽。 ✓ ○
5. 以思喜歡看時間短的運動比賽。 ✓ ○

Think & Discuss

Work in pairs and answer the questions in Chinese.

1. 為什麼以安說打籃球一定要合作才行？
2. 以安、以晴和以思喜歡什麼奧運比賽？
3. 你喜歡團隊運動還是個人運動？為什麼？

Culture Link

The Origins of the Olympic Games

The first Olympic Games were held in 776 BC. Since then, sports competitions were held at the temple of Zeus in Olympia, Greece, once every four years during the religious festivals to honor the Greek god Zeus. During that period, all states in war had to make peace with each other and weapons were prohibited in the Olympiad area; all paths leading to Olympia would be made accessible for all. Subsequently, the Olympic Games became a major event for all Greek states. The objectives of the ancient Olympic Games were twofold, one was to honor Zeus the king of the gods, the other was to promote peace and end wars and hatred. The winners of the athletic games were crowned with olive wreaths which symbolized hope and peace.

 Have you ever watched the Olympic Games? Which is your favorite sport? Why?

LESSON 8

1	接力賽不只要跑得快，接棒子(bàng zi)的時候還要接得好(jiē)，	因此(yīn cǐ)	選手(xuǎn shǒu)們還是需要練習很多次。
	政府給了爸爸失業金，		我們的生活沒有問題。

A: 旅行前要準備很多事，得花很多時間。

B: 出發前準備好，我們才能玩得開心、學得更多，因此(yīn cǐ)一定得花時間準備。

TIP This structure is used for expressing the cause and effect of a circumstance. The section after the word 因此 describes the outcome, while the preceding section indicates the cause or condition that leads to the outcome.

A: 沒想到我們學校的籃球(lán qiú)隊贏了。

B: 雖然我們的選手(xuǎn shǒu)投籃(tóu lán)沒有對手(duì shǒu)好，可是我們團隊(tuán duì)配合(pèi hé)得很好，因此(yīn cǐ)才能贏得比賽。

Using sentence structure 1, complete the dialogues with the helping phrases.

1. A: 你們今年為什麼沒有打算出國旅行？
   B: <u>爸爸失業了，東西越來越貴，因此我們得減少花費。</u>

   （失業／東西越來越貴／減少花費）

2. A: 我們的接力賽(jiē lì sài)選手(xuǎn shǒu)贏了比賽，還破紀錄(pò jì lù)了呢！
   B: <u>我們的選手每天練習，加上</u>

   （練習／團隊(tuán duì)合作／冠軍(guàn jūn)）

精彩的奧運

2	打籃球的時候，所有的球員(qiú yuán)	一定要	一起合作	才行。
	下個月的百米接力賽(bǎi mǐ jiē lì sài)		好好練習	

A: 明天的歷史考試，我把書看了兩遍了，還是背不起來。

B: 想要記住歷史一定要弄懂歷史事件才行。

A: 你覺得當學生會會長需要什麼能力？

B: 當學生會會長一定要做事負責、辦事能力強才行。

> **TIP**
> An event or a situation is stated before 一定要, while an essential condition relating to the event or situation is mentioned before 才行. Hence, the sentence structure refers to a particular situation where certain conditions have to be fulfilled in order to achieve the desired outcome stated earlier.

 Rewrite the sentences using sentence structure 2.

1. 公平(gōng píng)的人才能當裁判(cái pàn)。

   當裁判一定要公平才行。

2. 想要得到籃球(lán qiú)賽冠軍(guàn jūn)，球員(qiú yuán)就要團隊(tuán duì)合作。

   要得到籃球賽冠軍一定要團隊合作才行。

3. 出國旅行要配合放假的時間。

   ~~出國~~一定要配合放假的時間才行。

精彩的奧運

LESSON 8

Listening

Text > Dialogue section

SCENARIO: A sports competition took place in school today. 以晴 and her siblings return home to tell their mother the results of the competition.

 Listen to the Go700 CD-ROM for the dialogue and answer the following questions.

1. 以安今天參加什麼比賽？
   (A) lán qiú 籃球比賽 (B) 棒球比賽 (C) 桌球比賽

2. 是誰在比賽最後一秒得分？ miǎo dé fēn
   (A) 以安 (B) 以安的隊友 duì shǒu　qiú yuán (C) 對手的球員

3. 以安那一隊贏了對手幾分？ duì shǒu
   (A) 一分 (B) 三分 (C) 六分

4. 誰沒有看以安的比賽？
   (A) 以晴 (B) 媽媽 (C) 以思

5. 下面哪一個句子是對的？
   (A) 以思和以晴在操場上尖叫，因為哥哥贏球了。 jiān jiào
   (B) 以安是媽媽的新偶像，因為他的表現很好。 biǎo xiàn
   (C) 以安的班贏球了，班上的女生開心得又叫又跳。

New Words

miǎo 秒	seconds	duì yǒu 隊友	team mate
jiān jiào 尖叫	scream; shriek	biǎo xiàn 表現	performance; perform

精彩的奧運

B Number the following text in the correct order to form a coherent conversation.

1. 媽媽：以安，你的手跟腳怎麼了？

6. 以晴：對啊！就是因為那一球，哥哥他們那一隊才以 <u>68比67</u> 贏了對方。他們班的女生開心得又叫又跳，一直在尖叫！

4. 以晴：對啊！哥哥今天在最後十秒的時候，為了救球，<u>整個人摔倒在地上</u>，我都緊張死了。

2. 以安：我今天參加籃球比賽，<u>不小心摔傷的</u>，沒事。

7. 以思：對啊！吵得我的耳朵都快聽不到聲音了。

5. 以思：然後哥哥馬上<u>把球傳給隊友</u>，隊友就在最後一秒的時候投籃，沒想到球真的投進了，還是一個三分球！他們<u>配合得真好</u>！

8. 媽媽：媽媽<u>今天有事去不了</u>，不過 ❸ 哥哥今天的表現聽起來真是精彩極了！

3. 以思：媽，哥哥今天的籃球打得好棒，他是我的<u>新偶像</u>！

C Listen to the dialogue on the Go700 CD-ROM again, and fill in the blanks.

LESSON 8

3.
| 哥哥今天的表現 | 聽起來 | 真是精彩極了！ |
| 籃球是團隊合作的運動， | 打起來 | 很精彩。 |

biǎo xiàn / lán qiú tuán duì

A: 你覺得這件衣服怎麼樣？
B: 這件衣服你**穿起來**好看極了。

A: 為什麼你不喜歡跳水比賽？(tiào shuǐ)
B: 每場跳水比賽都差不多，**看起來**很無聊。

TIP: The phrase or sentence that follows "Verb + 起來" is the speaker's evaluation of the topic stated in front.

Using sentence structure 3, complete the dialogues with the helping phrases.

1. A: 爸爸從歐洲買回來的糖果好吃嗎？
   B: 我不太喜歡，_我不太喜歡，因為吃起來太甜了_ （太甜了）

2. A: 弟弟生病了，你知道嗎？
   B: 我知道，他的聲音_聽起來累極了_。 （累極了）

3. A: 體操很難學嗎？(tǐ cāo)
   B: _體操學起來不容易_，
   但是體操是我最喜歡的課外活動。 （不容易）

Go700 WANT TO LEARN MORE?
Check out the Text > Sentence Pattern section on the Go700 CD-ROM.

精彩的奧運

^{shèng bù jiāo   bài bù něi}
「勝不驕，敗不餒」
Not Conceited in Victory, and not Disheartened by Defeat

In Chinese, there is this saying "勝不驕，敗不餒", which means a person should not be proud of his or her success, and should not be disheartened when encountering failure or difficulties. This attitude should be adopted when one takes part in competitions or games, regardless of whether there are clear winners or losers. As success is only momentary and it is common for people to fail, winners should not look down on others, and those who fail should remain hopeful too. In the ancient days, "勝不驕，敗不餒" was used in the context of war, to remind the victorious side to remain humble, as their enemies could always turn the tables; it also encouraged the losing side not to lose heart as they would have a chance to fight back. In the modern times when wars are relatively uncommon, countries and groups of people engage in competitive sports and games. Hence, "勝不驕，敗不餒" becomes the best representation of good sportsmanship.

 Talk about the meaning of "勝不驕，敗不餒" and give an example.

Form groups of three and role-play the scenario. You may use the sentence structures provided below.

CHARACTERS:

爸爸, 以安, 以思

SCENARIO:

Father is discussing with the brothers about the tennis finals that took place in the afternoon. They talk about the importance of sportsmanship.

SENTENCE STRUCTURES:

1. ……，^{yīn cǐ}因此……
2. ……一定要……才行
3. ……Verb + 起來……
4. ……，得……
5. 要是……，怎麼辦？

LESSON 8

Learn about the Chinese Language & Culture

「比賽好不精彩」、「我好不快樂」，你看過這些句子嗎？你覺得比賽是「精彩」還是「不精彩」？說話的人是「快樂」還是「不快樂」？

我們不能從一句話就知道*答案，得從頭到尾把*文章都讀過，才知道作者是怎麼想的。中文很有趣，在*大多數的情形下「比賽好精彩」和「比賽好不精彩」意思是一樣的；「我好快樂」和「我好不快樂」說的都是很快樂的意思。中文的「不」在這裡沒有*負面的意思，「好不」*表達的是*肯定的、帶*感嘆的*語氣。

請你想想看，這些句子是負面的還是肯定的呢？

TIP 好不＝很

1. 我今天看了一場好精彩的球賽。（精彩/不精彩）
2. 這次的競選活動好不熱鬧。（熱鬧/不熱鬧）
3. 我覺得你一點都不獨立。（獨立/不獨立）
4. 明天就要出國旅行了，真讓人好不興奮啊！（興奮/不興奮）

*答案 answer　文章 article　大多數 majority　負面的 negative　表達 express
肯定的 affirmative　感嘆的 exclamatory　語氣 tone of voice

精彩的奧運

Work It Out

No matter who won or lost a competition, as long as all contestants gave their best, it is a good and exciting match. What are the words that you would use to describe an exciting match?

TASK
Be a Sports Commentator

1. Divide the students into 3 groups. Each group sends a representative to draw for the picture they need to work on.

2. Within the group, each student is to list words and sentence structures that can be used for describing the picture. Then, share them with other students, and note down words and sentence structures given by other students that are suitable.

3. Describe the picture in a short paragraph using the words and sentence structures gathered just now.

我的句子：_____

_____

_____

4. In turns, each student reads out his/her sentences to the class.

LEARNING LOG

I can…

		Excellent	Good	Fair	Need Improvement
1	explain the meaning of sportsmanship and team spirit.	○	○	○	○
2	describe the origins of the Olympic Games and my favorite Olympics sport and reasons for liking it.	○	○	○	○
3	use "……，因此……" to explain the cause and effect of events or situations.	○	○	○	○
4	use "……一定要……才行" to indicate a particular situation in which certain conditions must be fulfilled.	○	○	○	○
5	use "……Verb + 起來……" to evaluate a topic stated earlier.	○	○	○	○
6	use the word 不 to reinforce an affirmative expression.	○	○	○	○
7	write 團隊, 精神, 配合, and 因此.	○	○	○	○

LESSON 9

孔子
Confucius

1. Do you know whose statue this is?
2. What does the phrase 萬世師表 (wàn shì shī biǎo) mean?

1 Know Confucius and his school of thought
2 Clearly express the key point in one's opinion
3 Use an emphatic tone to express an uncommon situation
4 Know the *Analects of Confucius* and understand the meanings behind some of the quotes
5 Understand the cultural differences between how the East and West view and regard teachers

115

SCENARIO: 以晴 is sitting in the school field reading a book. 久美子 sees her and comes over for a chat.

A Complete the conversation by using the sentence structures provided.

久美子：以晴，妳在看什麼書？

以　晴：我在看《*孔子(kǒng zǐ)的故事》。

久美子：我知道孔子(kǒng zǐ)是一個老師，他想要和大家說說自己的想法，因此_____。

以　晴：這本書不但有好看的故事，還介紹了很多孔子(kǒng zǐ)的想法。像他說過：學過的知識_____。

久美子：他還說過：_____；別人做不好的，也要想想自己有沒有一樣的問題。

以　晴：沒錯！這本書我_____。

久美子：_____，回家之前我也要去買一本。

*孔子 Confucius

A. 一定要懂得用在生活上才行　　B. 越看越覺得很有意思
C. 聽起來這本書很有趣　　　　　D. 帶學生到處旅行
E. 我們應該學習別人好的地方

B In pairs, practice reading out the above conversation. Next, exchange roles and repeat the exercise.

LESSON 9

		wěi dà 偉大	wěi rén 偉人	xióng wěi 雄偉 (magnificent)	
	bì 必	bú bì 不必 (need not)		bì yào 必要 (necessary)	bì xū 必須 (essential)
rén ài 仁愛	lǐ / lǐ jié 禮／禮節	lǐ yí 禮儀 (etiquette)	zūn jìng 尊敬	zūn zhòng 尊重 (respect)	zhòng shì 重視 (value; regard highly)
xià qí 下棋	tiào qí 跳棋 (Chinese checkers)	xiàng qí 象棋 (Chinese chess)	wéi qí 圍棋 (Go chess)	qí mǎ 騎馬 (horse riding)	shè jiàn 射箭 (archery)
jūn zǐ 君子 (gentleman)	xiǎo rén 小人 (an evil person)	zhì shèng xiān shī 至聖先師 (the Great Sage and Teacher, a term for Confucius)		zūn shī zhòng dào 尊師重道 (respect the teacher and heed his teachings)	

New Words

wěi dà 偉大 | great; mighty	wěi rén 偉人 | a great man	bì 必 | must; surely
rén ài 仁愛 | benevolence and kindness	lǐ / lǐ jié 禮／禮節 | code of behavior; protocol	zūn jìng 尊敬 | honor; respect
xià qí 下棋 | play chess		

I am Confucius

1. The teacher prepares two sets of word cards and one Confucius card. The students sit in a circle and the teacher distributes two cards to each student. One of the students will receive the Confucius card.

2. Student A with the Confucius card has to stand up and say "我是孔子，我有X". The student with the X card will exchange it with Student A to get the Confucius card. Once Student A receives two identical word cards, he or she can paste them on the board and return to his or her seat.

3. Limit the card exchange to 5 seconds. The next student with the Confucius card will first read out the word on the board, followed by the word he or she is holding, "我是孔子，我有X、Y". The game continues in this manner.

4. If the student is unable to read out the word or pronounce it wrongly, the students will exchange their cards again.

孔子

SCENARIO: The teacher introduced a famous person in class today. After class, 以思 tells his family about this person.

以思一下課回家，就問：「今天老師說了一句很有意思的話。三個人走在一起，一定有我的老師。他說這是中國的Confucius說的，誰是Confucius啊？」

以晴聽了就對以思說：「我知道這句話！這句話的中文應該是『三人行，必有我師』。Confucius就是孔子，他很有名，他是一位老師。為了紀念孔子，孔子生日那一天，還有很多學生表演跳舞。」

爸爸說：「Confucius姓孔，是兩千五百年前的中國人。他是一位非常偉大的老師，大家都叫他『孔子』。兩千五百多年以前，他就有自己的學校，還帶著學生一邊旅行一邊上課。他有三千多個學生！」

以思說：「一邊旅行一邊上課，真是太棒了！兩千五百年前他教什麼？」媽媽說：「孔子是一位很有自己想法的老師，他用不同的方法教不同的學生，只要想學習的人都可以來找他。他教學生讀書跟做人的道理，①他認為『仁愛』和『禮節』最重要。心裡要有愛，對人要有禮。他還教學生*書寫、寫詩、唱歌、下棋。孔子不但是好老師，也是好學生，他很喜歡學習。他認為，三個人走在一起，除了自己以外，另外的兩位都是自己的老師。看到別人做得好的地方，要學習，所以他說『三人行，必有我師』。」

以思說：「孔子真能幹！上他的課一定很有趣！」接著他對以晴和以安說：「孔子說『三人行，必有我師』。你們兩個人，誰是我的老師啊？」

*書寫 refers to 寫字 (to write). During Confucius' days, paper was not invented yet and so people wrote on bamboo slips.

New Words

| kǒng zǐ 孔子 | Confucius | dào lǐ 道理 | truth; reason; sense | rèn wéi 認為 | think |

Exercises

Which is correct?

Which of the following statements about Confucius are correct?

☐ 1. 孔(kǒng)子(zǐ)是以思的老師。

☐ 2. 孔(kǒng)子(zǐ)是兩千五百年前的中國人。

☐ 3. 孔(kǒng)子(zǐ)一直在學習。

☐ 4. 孔(kǒng)子(zǐ)能用一個方法，教好每一個學生。

☐ 5. 孔(kǒng)子(zǐ)的學生會在生日那一天跳舞。

☐ 6. 孔(kǒng)子(zǐ)認(rèn)為(wéi)對人有禮(lǐ)、心裡有愛最重要。

☐ 7. 只要想學習的學生，孔(kǒng)子(zǐ)都會教。

☐ 8. 孔(kǒng)子(zǐ)很能幹，只有三個人可以當他的老師。

Think & Discuss

Work in pairs and answer the questions in Chinese.

1. 「三人行，必(bì)有我師」是什麼意思？

2. 孔(kǒng)子(zǐ)在兩千五百年前教什麼？

3. 如果你是孔(kǒng)子(zǐ)，你覺得以安和以晴，誰才是以思的老師？為什麼？

Confucianism

Confucius, hailed as one of the greatest teachers in China, is the founder of Confucianism and his teachings epitomize the Chinese cultural thought. His school of philosophy advocates virtues such as 仁義 (rén yì, benevolence and righteousness), 禮樂 (lǐ yuè, ceremonial rites and music), and 德治教化 (dé zhì jiào huà, moral education).

Not only did the Confucian thought shape the daily life and culture of Chinese people, it also influenced many people in other regions over the past 2000 years. For instance, Confucianism is widely practiced in Korea, where almost 80% of Koreans are either followers or are influenced by the Confucian thought. In Japan, Confucian ideas prevail in many aspects of the society, including politics, laws, religion, moral ethics, as well as the arts and literature. The influence of Confucianism, though varying through the ages, has never stopped, even until today. Regions around China, such as the Korean Peninsula, Japan and Vietnam, are strongly influenced by Confucianism and this has led to the formation of an East Asian Confucian cultural circle.

An Anecdote on Confucius

Confucius had a student named Yan Hui (顏回), who was also from the State of Lu (魯國) as Confucius. During that time, the different states were at war with each other and captive soldiers became slaves. There were many Lu soldiers who became slaves in the other states. In order to rescue them, the Lu government offered to compensate and reward anyone who managed to redeem these slaves.

Although Yan Hui redeemed many slaves from the State of Qi (齊國), he did not seek reimbursement and rewards, and with that he won the praises of the people. However, Confucius criticized him, "By not accepting compensation and rewards, you are indirectly causing distress to others in the State who wanted to rescue the slaves, and eventually no one would be willing to do that anymore." Yan Hui was shocked to see the repercussions of his actions. Confucius further explained, "You are rich and hence you can afford to rescue the slaves without having to claim rewards or reimbursement. However, the majority of the Lu people do not have the financial means to do so. When they approached the government for rewards and claims after redeeming the slaves, they will be compared unfavorably with you and could face discrimination. On the other hand, the financial burden will be too much for them to bear if they were to forgo compensation and rewards." When Yan Hui realized his error, he immediately went to claim his rewards and reimbursement.

Confucius is one of the greatest teachers in China. Are there any great teachers in your country?

Language Focus

	rèn wéi		
1	孔子	認為	「仁愛」和「禮節」 rén ài　　　lǐ jié	最重要。
	外公		學習做人的道理 　　　　dào lǐ	

A: 這次的中文考試，我表現不好，妳是怎麼準備的呢？

B: 學習語言，我 認為 方法 最重要 。
　　　　　rèn wéi

A: 我們快來不及了，為什麼爸爸開車開得這麼慢？

B: 因為爸爸 認為 交通安全 最重要 。
　　　　　rèn wéi

> **TIP:** The speaker uses the phrase 認為 to express an opinion which is made after analysis and deliberation, and the part before 最重要 is the key point among these considerations.

 Using sentence structure 1, complete the dialogues with the helping phrases.

1. A: 他們不可能贏了，為什麼還要繼續比賽？

   B: _____（運動精神）

2. A: 我和老師說話的時候都會注意禮儀。
   　　　　　　　　　　　　　　　lǐ yí

   B: _____（尊師重道）
   　　　　　　　　　　　　　　　zūn shī zhòng dào

3. A: 要是我學功夫，就沒有時間讀書了。

   B: 可是 _____（興趣）

4. A: 如果你失業了，怎麼辦？

   B: 如果我失業了，_____（減少花費）

122　孔子

LESSON 9

Listening

Text > Dialogue section

SCENARIO: 阿明, 張靜, 以晴, and 久美子 are leaving the classroom after lessons when they saw 方健 talking to the teacher. They come over to talk to 方健 after the teacher left.

A Listen to the Go700 CD-ROM for the dialogue and answer the following multiple-choice questions.

1. 為什麼方健常跟老師行禮(xíng lǐ)？
   (A) 是一個習慣(xí guàn) (B) 尊敬(zūn jìng)老師 (C) 他想要早點下課

2. 老師的地位(dì wèi)跟誰差不多？
   (A) 校長 (B) 父母 (C) 爺爺奶奶

3. 哪一個國家的人也知道孔子(kǒng zǐ)？
   (A) 印度 (B) 美國 (C) 日本

4. 如果很尊敬(zūn jìng)一個偉人(wěi rén)，會做什麼事？
   (A) 在很多地方放他的銅像(tóng xiàng)。
   (B) 常常向他行禮(xíng lǐ)。
   (C) 學他說話。

5. 下面哪一個句子是對的？
   (A) 方健在日本常常向老師行禮(xíng lǐ)。
   (B) 老師的地位(dì wèi)很高，所以和老師說話之後要行禮(xíng lǐ)。
   (C) 張靜覺得老師的地位(dì wèi)高，所以每一個老師都應該有自己的銅像(tóng xiàng)。

New Words

行禮 xíng lǐ — salute; pay respect	習慣 xí guàn — habit; be accustomed to	地位 dì wèi — position; status
節 jié — lesson period	銅像 tóng xiàng — bronze statue	

孔子

B Number the following text in the correct order to form a coherent conversation.

[1] 阿　　明：方健，為什麼你每次跟老師說完話，都要跟他們點頭行禮(xíng lǐ)說「謝謝」呢？

[ ] 方　　健：真的嗎？我沒注意到，＿＿＿＿＿＿＿＿＿＿＿＿＿＿＿＿，習慣(xí guàn)了。

[ ] 阿　　明：❷連日本人都知道他，那孔子(kǒng zǐ)真的是一位偉大(wěi dà)的老師！

[ ] 張　　靜：對啊！在中國，老師的地位(dì wèi)很高，就跟爸媽差不多，所以＿＿＿＿＿＿＿＿＿＿＿＿＿＿＿，都會行禮(xíng lǐ)說「謝謝」。

[ ] 張　　靜：應該是吧！在中國，孔子(kǒng zǐ)很有名。很多地方都有他的銅像(tóng xiàng)，這是＿＿＿＿＿＿＿的一種表現。

[ ] 方　　健：不只是說完話，每節(jié)課上課的時候，也要跟老師問好；到了下課的時候，還要跟老師說謝謝。還有，有的人即使在很遠的地方看到老師，也會行禮(xíng lǐ)，這是＿＿＿＿＿＿＿＿＿＿＿＿＿＿＿＿。

[ ] 以　　晴：這應該跟孔子(kǒng zǐ)有關係吧！孔子(kǒng zǐ)是大家都＿＿＿＿＿＿＿＿＿＿＿＿。

[ ] 久美子：孔子(kǒng zǐ)＿＿＿＿＿＿＿＿＿＿＿＿＿＿＿＿，在日本也是啊！

C Listen to the dialogue on the Go700 CD-ROM again, and fill in the blanks.

LESSON 9

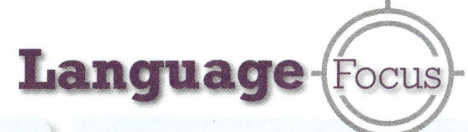

2	連	日本人	都	知道孔子(kǒng zǐ)。
		做菜		不會。

TIP: The situation stated after the word 連 is what the speaker thinks is uncommon. The sentence structure indicates an emphatic tone, and the emphasized section is placed between the words 連 and 都.

A: 孔子(kǒng zǐ)是很有名的偉人(wěi rén)嗎？

B: 很有名，連小孩子都知道孔子(kǒng zǐ)的故事。

A: 為什麼你弟弟看起來這麼累？

B: 他很忙，連星期天都去學騎馬(qí mǎ)。

 Using sentence structure 2, complete the dialogues with the helping phrases.

1. A: 這個數學問題看起來不難。

   B: _____（妹妹）

2. A: 你怎麼知道我喜歡聽中文歌？

   B: _____（洗澡）

3. A: 我不會象棋(xiàng qí)，我還是玩電腦遊戲好了。

   B: _____，你不想學嗎？（弟弟）

4. A: 你現在每天都要打工嗎？

   B: 對啊！_____（假日）

Check out the Text > Sentence Pattern section on the Go700 CD-ROM.

孔子

How Chinese Regard Teachers?

Do you know what the students in the picture are doing?

Since ancient times, Chinese people have held teachers in high regard, seeing them as having the same level of importance as Heaven, Earth, and parents. Hence, teaching is not just a normal job, but one with an elevated social status. Before lessons begin, the students have to be seated at their place to await the teacher's arrival. As the teacher walks into class, the class representative will give a command "起立" (qǐ lì, class stand) and the whole class will rise to greet the teacher "老師好". They can only sit after the teacher gives them the permission to do so. In the West, these practices are uncommon, and students do not have to stand and greet their teachers. Also, students do not stay in a fixed classroom all the day, as they usually move around different classrooms attending lessons taught by different teachers. Each student has a different class schedule, so the lesson venue and the teacher will be different.

 In your country, do you have to greet your teachers before class? If you happen to see your teachers outside school, how do you greet them?

Form groups of four and role-play the scenario. You may use the sentence structures provided below.

CHARACTERS:

爸爸, 以安, 以晴, 以思

SCENARIO:

Father is discussing with the children about what makes a good teacher.

SENTENCE STRUCTURES:

1. ……認為(rèn wéi)……最重要
2. 連……都……
3. 即使……，也……
4. ……，因此……
5. ……一定要……才行
6. …… Verb + 起來……

孔子

LESSON 9

Learn about the Chinese Language & Culture

　　有一個人很有名，只要是學中文的人都認識他，這個人就是「孔(kǒng)子(zǐ)」。大家*尊(zūn)稱(chēng)他為「至(zhì)聖(shèng)先(xiān)師(shī)」。

　　孔(kǒng)子(zǐ)去過很多地方，跟很多人說他的想法，希望大家能用他的方法來*治(zhì)理(lǐ)國家。很多人很尊(zūn)敬(jìng)孔(kǒng)子(zǐ)，也有很多人從不同的地方來，想當孔(kǒng)子(zǐ)的學生，跟著他到各地去旅行。

　　孔(kǒng)子(zǐ)的學生把孔(kǒng)子(zǐ)說過的話，記錄下來，變成了《*論(lún)語(yǔ)》這本書。你知道下面這幾句話的意思嗎？

1. 三人行，必(bì)有我師（每個人都有可以學習的地方，我們要學習別人好的地方，*改(gǎi)正(zhèng)我們自己不好的地方。）

2. 知之為知之，不知為不知，是知也（真的知道就說知道，不知道的事就說不知道，這才是真正的知道。）

3. 己所不*欲(yù)，*勿(wù)*施(shī)於人（自己不喜歡的東西，不要給別人。）

4. 三思而後行（做事之前要先想清楚再做。）

5. *非(fēi)禮(wù)勿視，非(fēi)禮(wù)勿聽，非(fēi)禮(wù)勿言，非(fēi)禮(wù)勿動（不合禮(lǐ)節(jié)規(guī)定(dìng)的事不要看，不合禮節規定的話不要聽，不合禮節規定的話不要說，不合禮節規定的事不要做。）

---

*尊稱 address respectfully　　治理 govern; manage　　論語 the Analects of Confucius　　改正 correct

欲 want; desire　　勿 do not　　施 impose　　非 not　　規定 rules; regulations

孔子

Work It Out

Confucius is China's most famous teacher with his own school of thought. If Confucius were to come to the modern world, do you think he will still be a good teacher? Or are there any other jobs that are more suitable for him?

TASK: Finding Confucius a Job

1. Divide the class into groups. Based on the stories of Confucius and his sayings, each group will have to write an introduction of Confucius in Chinese, so as to find a suitable job for him.

2. The introduction has to include the job that the group is seeking for Confucius, and the reason why he is suitable for the job.

3. Each group will then send one representative to present what they think Confucius should be working as.

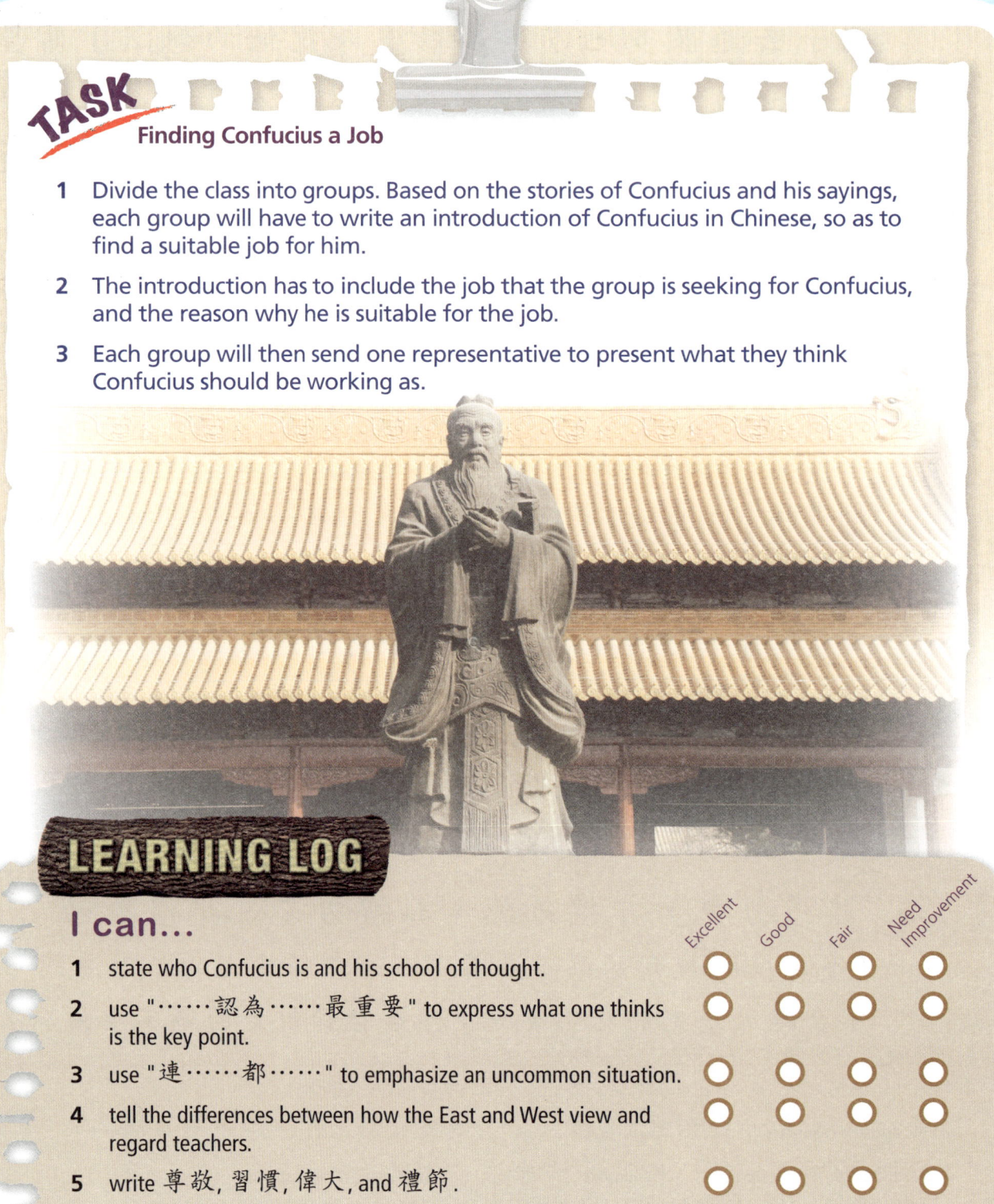

LEARNING LOG

I can...

		Excellent	Good	Fair	Need Improvement
1	state who Confucius is and his school of thought.	○	○	○	○
2	use "……認為……最重要" to express what one thinks is the key point.	○	○	○	○
3	use "連……都……" to emphasize an uncommon situation.	○	○	○	○
4	tell the differences between how the East and West view and regard teachers.	○	○	○	○
5	write 尊敬, 習慣, 偉大, and 禮節.	○	○	○	○

LESSON 10

端午節
The Dragon Boat Festival

1 Have you ever eaten the food shown in the picture?
2 Do you know what the people above are doing?
3 When are these activities held?

1 Know the activities and customs of the Dragon Boat Festival
2 Express the targets met or actions taken after certain conditions are fulfilled
3 Explain the objective of a topic
4 Describe a situation in which there are no exceptions
5 Understand the poem about the Dragon Boat Festival in the lesson

Get Started

A Rearrange the following sentences in the correct order to form a coherent passage.

A 是為了紀念中國一位偉人。華人認為過節的時候，

B 對華人來說，一年有三個重要的節日。除了過年、中秋節以外，

C 非常有意思，所以現在連外國人都知道這個節日。

D *端午節(duān wǔ jié)也是重要的節日。端午節(duān wǔ jié)在每年的農曆五月五日，

E 也會回家過節。另外，過端午節(duān wǔ jié)的時候，有一些特別的食物與習慣，

F 全家人在一起最重要，因此，有的人即使在很遠的地方工作，

*端午節 Dragon Boat Festival

The correct order of the sentences is:

B → D → A → F → E → C

B In pairs, practice reading out the above sentences in the correct order.

LESSON 10

huá chuán	lóng zhōu sài	dǎ gǔ
划船	龍舟賽	打鼓

zòng zi	xiāng bāo
粽子	香包 (scent pouch)

gǔ shǒu	qí zi
鼓手 (drummer)	旗子

ài cǎo	xí sú
艾草 (mugwort; wormwood plant)	習俗 (custom)

guó wáng	shì zhǎng
國王	市長

hé	hé liú
河	河流 (rivers)

rén mín	guó qí
人民	國旗 (country flag)

shuǐ shàng yùn dòng
水上運動

huà lóng diǎn jīng	xǔ xǔ rú shēng
畫龍點睛 (add a finishing touch)	栩栩如生 (life-like)

chōng làng	qián shuǐ
衝浪 (surfing)	潛水 (diving)

New Words

huá chuán 划船	row a boat	lóng zhōu sài 龍舟賽	dragon boat competition	dǎ gǔ 打鼓	play the drum
qí zi 旗子	flag	zòng zi 粽子	Chinese glutinous rice dumpling	guó wáng 國王	king
shì zhǎng 市長	mayor	rén mín 人民	people	hé 河	river
shuǐ shàng yùn dòng 水上運動	water sport				

Snatch the Flag

1. The class is split into the red and yellow team. Each team will have their own team flag.
2. The teacher places the red team flag at the starting point of the yellow team and vice versa. All students will have a word card hanging on them.
3. Upon hearing the whistle (blew by the teacher), each team sends a student to the front. As the opponents meet, they have to read out their own word followed by the word of the student in the opposite team. The slower student to do so will be eliminated and the next student from that group will take over. If the two students read out their words at the same time, the winner will be determined through a finger-guessing game.
4. The team that eliminates all their opponents and grab their flag wins the game.

端午節

Reading

Text > Reading section

> **SCENARIO:** The Dragon Boat Festival is coming soon and the school is organizing some activities for the occasion. What are these activities? Are 以安, 以晴, and 以思 participating in them?

吃晚飯的時候，以安很高興地告訴大家，他報名參加了今年的龍舟賽，從下週起，每個星期六都要去練習，六月要比賽。爸爸笑著說：「我以前也參加過龍舟賽，這是很好的水上運動。」

以思問以安：「什麼是龍舟賽？」

以晴說：「我知道！龍舟賽就是划龍船比賽。在中文學校上課的時候，我看過划龍船的影片。龍船很長，上面坐著好多人，有的人坐在左邊，有的人坐在右邊，大家一邊划，一邊大聲叫。船上有人打鼓，還有一個人站在龍船的最前面，❶哪一隊先拿到旗子就贏了。老師還說，划龍船跟端午節有關。」

以思說：「我知道！端午節就是粽子節，我們要吃粽子。可是，為什麼要吃粽子，還要划龍船？」

媽媽告訴他們，❷端午節是為了紀念一位中國詩人。兩千多年以前，有一位詩人，他非常愛自己的國家，寫了很多愛國的詩，也希望國王能用心為人民做事。可是，這個國王不喜歡他，只聽壞人的話。這位詩人看到人民不快樂，心裡非常難過。有一天，他覺得自己沒有辦法幫助人民，就跳到河裡去。人民很喜歡這位詩人，一聽到他跳河，就趕快划船去救他；一邊打鼓，一邊把包好的飯丟到河裡餵魚，希望河裡的魚不要吃他。他死的那一天，是農曆的五月五日。後來，為了紀念這位詩人，大家在這一天划龍船，還有吃粽子。

以安說：「老師說，划龍船的那天，要請市長畫龍的眼睛，龍有了眼睛，看得到前面，龍船才能划得快。」以思說：「真有趣！以安比賽那一天，我們要一邊吃粽子，一邊幫以安加油！」

New Words

bào míng 報名 sign up for	huá 划 row	lóng chuán 龍船 dragon boat	yǐng piàn 影片 film
duān wǔ jié 端午節 Dragon Boat Festival	shī rén 詩人 poet	bàn fǎ 辦法 method; means	bāo 包 wrap

端午節

Exercises

True or False?

Answer the questions according to the reading passage.　　　　　　　　　　　　對　錯

1. 以安這個星期六要參加划_{huá}龍_{lóng}船_{chuán}比賽。　　　　○　✓

2. 龍_{lóng}舟_{zhōu}賽_{sài}和吃粽_{zòng}子_{zi}都是端_{duān}午_{wǔ}節_{jié}的活動。　　　✓　○

3. 以前的人把粽_{zòng}子_{zi}丟進河_{hé}裡，是為了給死去的詩_{shī}人_{rén}吃。　　　○　✓

4. 以前的人一邊打_{dǎ}鼓_{gǔ}一邊划_{huá}船_{chuán}是為了救詩_{shī}人_{rén}。　✓　○

5. 市_{shì}長_{zhǎng}給龍船_{lóng chuán}畫_{huà}龍的眼睛，是為了讓龍船_{lóng chuán}划_{huá}得更快。　✓　○

6. 以思想看以安的龍_{lóng}舟_{zhōu}比賽，因為去加油的人有粽_{zòng}子_{zi}吃。　○　✓

Think & Discuss

Work in pairs and answer the questions in Chinese.

1. 為什麼會有端_{duān}午_{wǔ}節_{jié}？

2. 人_{rén}民_{mín}為什麼要把包_{bāo}好的飯丟到河_{hé}裡？

3. 你看過龍_{lóng}舟_{zhōu}賽_{sài}或吃過粽_{zòng}子_{zi}嗎？你覺得怎麼樣？

Qu Yuan (屈原 Qū Yuán), the Patriotic Poet

Qu Yuan (屈原) was a court official in the State of Chu (楚國). As he was intelligent, patriotic, and had a flair for poetry writing, the King of Chu held him in high regard and appointed him to high-ranking positions. However, as Qu Yuan always pointed out unflattering truths to the King, and jealous court officials slandered him before the king, Qu Yuan's proposals were gradually unheeded by the King.

During that time, the rivaling State of Qin (秦國) who had always wanted to conquer the State of Chu pretended to forge an alliance with the latter. Qu Yuan saw through their guise and tried to convince the King of Chu not to believe the King of Qin. However, this angered the King of Chu who eventually banished Qu Yuan to the countryside. During the exile, Qu Yuan witnessed how his country was growing weaker and the people were living in distress. As he felt he could no longer contribute to the country, and not able to bear the sight of his country collapsing, he carried a big rock and threw himself into a river on the 5th day of lunar month of May.

When villagers nearby heard of what he did, they set out on boats to search for his body. Their search was futile. As the villagers were worried about his body being consumed by fish and shrimps, they wrapped rice using leaves and threw the dumplings into the river while sounding the drums and gongs to drive away the fish. Due to the great respect people had for Qu Yuan, they commemorated his death anniversary by the river every year on the 5th day of the lunar month of May. As time passes, the rowing of dragon boats as well as the wrapping of rice dumplings become the customary practice during the festival.

1. If you were Qu Yuan, what would you do?
2. In your country, are there any historical figures who were as patriotic as Qu Yuan and earned the respect of the people?

端午節

Language Focus

1	哪一隊	先拿到旗子(qí zi)	就	贏。
	什麼時候	有空		過去。

A: 誰可以得到禮物？
B: **哪一個人**會打鼓(dǎ gǔ)**就**可以得到禮物。

A: 我們買什麼紀念品給爸媽？
B: **什麼東西**適合爸媽，我們**就**買給他們當紀念品。

> **TIP**
> The question words (such as 哪, 誰, 什麼) at the start of the sentences are pronouns. The conditions that have to be fulfilled are stated after the question words, and the target met or action taken is indicated after the word 就.

Using sentence structure 1, complete the dialogues with the helping phrases.

1. A: 這次的龍舟賽(lóng zhōu sài)，哪一隊會贏？
   B: 哪一隊有團隊精神就能贏得比賽。 （團隊精神）

2. A: 你覺得誰能做鼓手(gǔ shǒu)的工作？
   B: 誰打鼓的能力好就能做這個工作。 （能力好）

3. A: 你想去哪一個國家旅行？
   B: _____ （美麗的風景）

4. A: 這一次的選舉，你要投給誰？
   B: _____ （負責任）

端午節

LESSON 10

2

端午節 (duān wǔ jié)	是為了	紀念一位中國詩人 (shī rén)。
教師節		紀念孔子。

A: 市長 (shì zhǎng) 為什麼常常舉辦介紹工作的活動？

B: 市長 (shì zhǎng) 舉辦介紹工作的活動**是為了**幫助失業的人。

TIP: The topic is stated before 是為了, while the aim of the topic is stated after it.

A: 聽說家明要去歐洲。

B: 他去歐洲**是為了**找在那裡讀書的姐姐。

PRACTICE IT

Using sentence structure 2, complete the dialogues with the helping phrases.

1. A: 為什麼你那麼喜歡潛水 (qián shuǐ)？

    B: 我 _____ （看海洋生物）

2. A: 你買這些葉子要做什麼？

    B: _____ （包粽子 bāo zòng zi）

3. A: 為什麼你的社區常常辦拍賣會？

    B: _____ （做環保）

4. A: 為什麼你要學這麼多語言？

    B: _____ （增加語文能力）

端午節

Listening

Text > Dialogue section

SCENARIO: 以晴, 以思, and their mother are busy preparing the items for the Dragon Boat Festival. What are they doing?

A Listen to the Go700 CD-ROM for the dialogue and answer the following multiple-choice questions.

1. 誰不想包<ruby>粽子<rt>bāo zòng zi</rt></ruby>了？
   (A) 媽媽　(B) 以晴　(C) 以思

2. 誰要負責清理廚房？
   (A) 媽媽　(B) 以晴　(C) 以思

3. 以晴家沒有<ruby>包<rt>bāo</rt></ruby>什麼<ruby>口味<rt>kǒu wèi</rt></ruby>的<ruby>粽子<rt>zòng zi</rt></ruby>？
   (A) 辣的　(B) 甜的　(C) <ruby>鹹<rt>xián</rt></ruby>的

4. 以思為什麼喜歡過節？
   (A) 因為有好玩的活動。
   (B) 因為有好吃的東西。
   (C) 因為有好聽的故事。

5. 下面哪一個句子是對的？
   (A) 以晴<ruby>包粽子<rt>bāo zòng zi</rt></ruby>包得很漂亮，因為她每年都在<ruby>包粽子<rt>bāo zòng zi</rt></ruby>。
   (B) 他們<ruby>包<rt>bāo</rt></ruby>了兩種不同<ruby>口味<rt>kǒu wèi</rt></ruby>的<ruby>粽子<rt>zòng zi</rt></ruby>。
   (C) 媽媽以前也沒<ruby>包<rt>bāo</rt></ruby>過<ruby>粽子<rt>zòng zi</rt></ruby>，自己練習以後，現在<ruby>包<rt>bāo</rt></ruby>得又快又好。

New Words

<ruby>口味<rt>kǒu wèi</rt></ruby>	flavor
<ruby>鹹<rt>xián</rt></ruby>	savory
<ruby>肉<rt>ròu</rt></ruby>	meat

LESSON 10

B Number the following text in the correct order to form a coherent conversation.

3 媽媽：❸什麼事情都需要練習的，媽媽以前常包粽子，現在當然可以包得 <u>又快又好</u> 。

4 以思：吃粽子很容易，<u>包粽子真麻煩</u> 。媽，我不想包了，我只想吃，可以嗎？

1 媽媽：以晴、以思，你們的粽子包好了沒？

6 以思：為了吃粽子，整理廚房當然沒問題！

9 以思：<u>中國人真有意思</u>，不管過什麼節，都會有好東西吃！像新年的 <u>年糕</u> 、中秋節的 <u>月餅</u> ，還有端午節的粽子，我最喜歡過節了！

7 以晴：這兩種粽子看起來都好好吃，<u>一種是甜的</u>一種是包肉的。對不對？

2 以晴：<u>用葉子包粽子真麻</u>。我包的粽子一點都不好看。媽，為什麼妳的粽子包得這麼漂亮？

8 媽媽：<u>中國地方大</u> ，每個地方的粽子都不一樣。<u>甜的</u>、<u>辣的</u> 都有。

5 媽媽：我和以晴負責包粽子，你要負責把廚房整理乾淨。

C Listen to the dialogue on the Go700 CD-ROM again, and fill in the blanks.

端午節

Customs of the Dragon Boat Festival

Putting Eggs Upright at Noon

The custom of putting eggs upright during the Dragon Boat Festival has been passed down through the generations. It is believed that making an egg stand upright can be most easily done on the day of the Dragon Boat Festival. From a scientific perspective, as the sun is directly shining on the Northern Hemisphere in this period, and with the sun and earth exerting gravitational forces in opposite directions, an egg can easily stand upright. You can try making an egg stand upright on the Dragon Boat Festival and see whether this belief is true.

Hanging Wormwood Plant/Mugwort on the Door

The Dragon Boat Festival falls on the lunar month of May when the weather is humid, warm, and stuffy. Such weather makes people uncomfortable and causes all kinds of pests to breed rapidly. These can lead to diseases and plants such as mugwort are used to get rid of the pests and ward off evil.

 In your country, are there any festivals that have special customs?

3

什麼	事情	都	需要練習。
	電視節目		喜歡看。

A: 誰可以參加龍舟賽(lóng zhōu sài)？

B: 什麼人都可以參加龍舟賽(lóng zhōu sài)。

A: 水上運動(shuǐ shàng yùn dòng)很危險，怎麼會有人想學？

B: 什麼水上運動(shuǐ shàng yùn dòng)都有人學。

> **TIP** The section "什麼 + Noun" is used to indicate any items in a certain category, and the word 都 indicates that there is no exception. Hence, this structure is used to indicate a situation in which there is no exception.

Rewrite the sentences using sentence structure 3.

1. 他把動物都畫得栩栩如生(xǔ xǔ rú shēng)。

___

2. 哥哥每一種口味(kǒu wèi)的粽子(zòng zi)都包(bāo)得很好。

___

3. 姊姊把所有事情都處理得很好，讓人尊敬。

___

4. 每個人都可以競選市長(shì zhǎng)。

___

Check out the Text > Sentence Pattern section on the Go700 CD-ROM.

端午節

Role Playing

Form groups of five and role-play the scenario. You may use the sentence structures provided below.

CHARACTERS:

爸爸, 媽媽, 以安, 以晴, 以思

SCENARIO:

以安 took part in a dragon boat competition in the morning and the whole family were there to support him. Over dinner, the family talks about the event.

SENTENCE STRUCTURES:

1. (Question Word)……就……
2. 什麼……都……
3. ……是為了……
4. 連……都……
5. 即使……，也……
6. ……一定要……才行

Learn about the Chinese Language & Culture

LESSON 10

端午節的時候，華人除了吃粽子、划龍舟紀念*屈原之外，還有很多有趣的習俗和活動。有人把端午節的習俗寫成一首詩：

> 五月五，過端午，
> 賽龍舟，*敲鑼鼓，
> 包粽子，*插艾蒲，
> 紀念屈原也*祈福。
> 喝*雄黃，把*蟲除；
> 取*井水，正中午；
> 立*雞蛋，*莫心浮；
> 端午習俗*傳千古。

你發現了嗎？這首詩很多句子最後一個字的*韻母都是「u」。在詩中句子的最後一個字，用韻母一樣或很像的字，就叫*押韻。押韻可以讓詩容易念，也容易記。

再念一念這首詩，你可以說出押韻的字是哪些嗎？請把這些字的拼音寫下來。

☐、☐、☐、☐、☐、☐、☐、☐

*屈原 Qu Yuan　　敲鑼鼓 sound the drum and gong　　插艾蒲 decorate with mugwort and calamus
祈福 pray for blessings　　雄黃 realgar　　蟲 bug　　井水 well water　　雞蛋 egg　　莫心浮 not to be impatient
傳千古 passed down through the years　　韻母 (phonetic) final　　押韻 rhyme

端午節

Work It Out

The Dragon Boat Festival is one of the three major festivals celebrated by Chinese people. Do you know of any other major festivals celebrated around the world and how are they celebrated?

TASK: Introducing Festivals around the World

1. The teacher guides students to name the major festivals celebrated around the world, and lists them on the board in chronological order of the month in which they are celebrated.

2. After selecting six festivals with the class, divide the students into six groups, each to be in charge of introducing one of the festivals. The introduction can include:
   (1) Origins of the festival;
   (2) Special food items made during the festival;
   (3) The activities held during the festival;
   (4) Special customs;
   (5) The venue, etc.

3. Each group presents a festival in the class, and the presentation methods should be varied to include posters, videos, performances, etc.

4. Finally, students vote for three festivals that they would like to take part in, as well as the group that gave the best presentation.

LEARNING LOG

I can...	Excellent	Good	Fair	Need Improvement
1 tell the activities held during the Dragon Boat Festival, and the origins of the customs.	○	○	○	○
2 use "(Question Word)……就……" to express the target met or actions taken once the conditions are fulfilled.	○	○	○	○
3 use "……是為了……" to express the objective of a certain topic.	○	○	○	○
4 use "什麼……都……" to express that there are no exceptions within a category.	○	○	○	○
5 understand and recite a poem about the Dragon Boat Festival.	○	○	○	○
6 write 人民, 划船, 打鼓, and 肉.	○	○	○	○

端午節

Vocabulary Index

Words marked with an asterisk (*) are supplementary vocabulary from each lesson. They are included to supplement students' vocabulary and enhance their oral proficiency.

Pinyin	Bopomofo	Traditional Character	English	Simplified Character	Lesson
A					
ài cǎo	ㄞˋ ㄘㄠˇ	艾草*	mugwort; wormwood plant	艾草	L10
ān pái	ㄢ ㄆㄞˊ	安排	arrange		L6
áo yè	ㄠˊ ㄧㄝˋ	熬夜*	work late into the night		L2
ào yùn	ㄠˋ ㄩㄣˋ	奧運	Olympic Games	奥运	L8
B					
bǎi mǐ	ㄅㄞˇ ㄇㄧˇ	百米	100 meters		L8
bàn fǎ	ㄅㄢˋ ㄈㄚˇ	辦法	method; means	办法	L10
bāng zhù	ㄅㄤ ㄓㄨˋ	幫助	help	帮助	L5
bàng zi	ㄅㄤˋ ˙ㄗ	棒子	baton		L8
bāo	ㄅㄠ	包	wrap		L10
bǎo xiǎn	ㄅㄠˇ ㄒㄧㄢˇ	保險*	insurance	保险	L6
bào míng	ㄅㄠˋ ㄇㄧㄥˊ	報名	sign up for	报名	L10
bào zhù	ㄅㄠˋ ㄓㄨˋ	抱住	hug		L7
běi ōu	ㄅㄟˇ ㄡ	北歐	Northern Europe	北欧	L1
běn lái	ㄅㄣˇ ㄌㄞˊ	本來	originally	本来	L5
bǐ jì	ㄅㄧˇ ㄐㄧˋ	筆記	notes	笔记	L3
bǐ jiào	ㄅㄧˇ ㄐㄧㄠˋ	比較	quite; relatively	比较	L4
bǐ shì	ㄅㄧˇ ㄕˋ	筆試*	written examination	笔试	L2
bì	ㄅㄧˋ	必	must; surely		L9
bì xū	ㄅㄧˋ ㄒㄩ	必須*	essential		L9
bì yào	ㄅㄧˋ ㄧㄠˋ	必要*	necessary		L9
biǎo xiàn	ㄅㄧㄠˇ ㄒㄧㄢˋ	表現	performance; perform	表现	L8
biǎo yǎn	ㄅㄧㄠˇ ㄧㄢˇ	表演	performance		L1
biàn	ㄅㄧㄢˋ	遍	(to indicate the number of times an action/state occurs) time	遍	L2
biàn lì	ㄅㄧㄢˋ ㄌㄧˋ	便利	convenient		L1
bǐng gōng wú sī	ㄅㄧㄥˇ ㄍㄨㄥ ㄨˊ ㄙ	秉公無私*	handle matters impartially	秉公无私	L5
bó wù guǎn	ㄅㄛˊ ㄨˋ ㄍㄨㄢˇ	博物館*	museum	博物馆	L1

Vocabulary Index 145

bú bì	ㄅㄨˊ ㄅㄧˋ	不必*	need not		L9
bù zé shǒu duàn	ㄅㄨˋ ㄗㄜˊ ㄕㄡˇ ㄉㄨㄢˋ	不擇手段*	resort to unscrupulous means	不择手段	L5

C

cái pàn	ㄘㄞˊ ㄆㄢˋ	裁判*	referee; umpire		L8
cái yuán	ㄘㄞˊ ㄩㄢˊ	裁員*	retrench; lay off	裁员	L7
cāo chǎng	ㄘㄠ ㄔㄤˇ	操場	sports ground	操场	L1
chá	ㄔㄚˊ	查	check		L6
chā	ㄔㄚ	差	differ		L4
chéng zhǎng	ㄔㄥˊ ㄓㄤˇ	成長	grow up	成长	L1
chí dào	ㄔˊ ㄉㄠˋ	遲到*	be late for (school, work, etc.)	迟到	L2
chōng làng	ㄔㄨㄥ ㄌㄤˋ	衝浪*	surfing	冲浪	L10
chū fā	ㄔㄨ ㄈㄚ	出發	set out; depart	出发	L6
chuán	ㄔㄨㄢˊ	船	boat; ship		L3
cū xīn	ㄘㄨ ㄒㄧㄣ	粗心*	careless		L2
cún qián	ㄘㄨㄣˊ ㄑㄧㄢˊ	存錢*	save money	存钱	L7

D

dǎ gǔ	ㄉㄚˇ ㄍㄨˇ	打鼓	play the drum		L10
dǎ suàn	ㄉㄚˇ ㄙㄨㄢˋ	打算	plan		L7
dà xià	ㄉㄚˋ ㄒㄧㄚˋ	大廈	building	大厦	L6
dà zì rán	ㄉㄚˋ ㄗˋ ㄖㄢˊ	大自然	nature		L1
dài biǎo	ㄉㄞˋ ㄅㄧㄠˇ	代表*	represent		L2
dān dú	ㄉㄢ ㄉㄨˊ	單獨*	alone; solitary	单独	L4
dāng xīn	ㄉㄤ ㄒㄧㄣ	當心	be careful of	当心	L3
dāng xuǎn	ㄉㄤ ㄒㄩㄢˇ	當選	be elected	当选	L5
dào lǐ	ㄉㄠˋ ㄌㄧˇ	道理	truth; reason; sense	道理	L9
dé fēn	ㄉㄜˊ ㄈㄣ	得分	score		L8
dēng jì	ㄉㄥ ㄐㄧˋ	登記*	register	登记	L6
dì diǎn	ㄉㄧˋ ㄉㄧㄢˇ	地點	site; location	地点	L6
dì wèi	ㄉㄧˋ ㄨㄟˋ	地位	position; status	地位	L9
diào	ㄉㄧㄠˋ	掉	fall; drop		L3
dōng fāng	ㄉㄨㄥ ㄈㄤ	東方	East; Oriental	东方	L6
dòng zuò	ㄉㄨㄥˋ ㄗㄨㄛˋ	動作	action	动作	L8
dú lì	ㄉㄨˊ ㄌㄧˋ	獨立	independent	独立	L4

Pinyin	Zhuyin	Traditional	English	Simplified	Lesson
dú zì	ㄉㄨˊ ㄗˋ	獨自*	alone	独自	L4
duān wǔ jié	ㄉㄨㄢ ㄨˇ ㄐㄧㄝˊ	端午節	Dragon Boat Festival	端午节	L10
duǎn jù	ㄉㄨㄢˇ ㄐㄩˋ	短劇	short play; skit	短剧	L5
duì shǒu	ㄉㄨㄟˋ ㄕㄡˇ	對手	opponent	对手	L8
duì yǒu	ㄉㄨㄟˋ ㄧㄡˇ	隊友	team mate	队友	L8
duì zhǎng	ㄉㄨㄟˋ ㄓㄤˇ	隊長	captain	队长	L8

E

Pinyin	Zhuyin	Traditional	English	Simplified	Lesson
è mèng	ㄜˋ ㄇㄥˋ	惡夢*	nightmare	恶梦	L2

F

Pinyin	Zhuyin	Traditional	English	Simplified	Lesson
fàn guī	ㄈㄢˋ ㄍㄨㄟ	犯規*	foul	犯规	L8
fáng huá	ㄈㄤˊ ㄏㄨㄚˊ	防滑	anti-slip	防滑	L3
fáng shài	ㄈㄤˊ ㄕㄞˋ	防晒	sunscreen		L3
fáng shài yóu	ㄈㄤˊ ㄕㄞˋ ㄧㄡˊ	防晒油	sunscreen lotion		L3
fáng shuǐ	ㄈㄤˊ ㄕㄨㄟˇ	防水	waterproof		L3
fàng sōng	ㄈㄤˋ ㄙㄨㄥ	放鬆*	relax	放松	L1
fēi pán	ㄈㄟ ㄆㄢˊ	飛盤	flying disc; Frisbee	飞盘	L4
fēn shù	ㄈㄣ ㄕㄨˋ	分數*	grade; score	分数	L2
fēng jǐng	ㄈㄥ ㄐㄧㄥˇ	風景	scenery	风景	L1
fù xí	ㄈㄨˋ ㄒㄧˊ	複習*	review	复习	L2
fù zá	ㄈㄨˋ ㄗㄚˊ	複雜*	complicated	复杂	L5
fù zé	ㄈㄨˋ ㄗㄜˊ	負責	be responsible for	负责	L5

G

Pinyin	Zhuyin	Traditional	English	Simplified	Lesson
gān / gān gān de	ㄍㄢ / ㄍㄢ ㄍㄢ ˙ㄉㄜ	乾/乾乾的*	dry	干/干干的	L3
gǎn kuài	ㄍㄢˇ ㄎㄨㄞˋ	趕快	hurry	赶快	L3
gè guó	ㄍㄜˋ ㄍㄨㄛˊ	各國	various countries	各国	L1
gū dān	ㄍㄨ ㄉㄢ	孤單*	lonely	孤单	L4
gǔ lǎo	ㄍㄨˇ ㄌㄠˇ	古老	ancient		L6
gǔ lì	ㄍㄨˇ ㄌㄧˋ	鼓勵*	encourage	鼓励	L8
gǔ shǒu	ㄍㄨˇ ㄕㄡˇ	鼓手*	drummer		L10
gù xiāng	ㄍㄨˋ ㄒㄧㄤ	故鄉	hometown	故乡	L4
guān guāng	ㄍㄨㄢ ㄍㄨㄤ	觀光*	sightseeing	观光	L1
guān guāng kè	ㄍㄨㄢ ㄍㄨㄤ ㄎㄜˋ	觀光客	tourists	观光客	L1
guǎn	ㄍㄨㄢˇ	管	manage		L5

Vocabulary Index

guàn jūn	ㄍㄨㄢˋ ㄐㄩㄣ	冠軍*	champion	冠军	L8
gōng chǐ	ㄍㄨㄥ ㄔˇ	公尺	meter		L8
gōng fū	ㄍㄨㄥ ㄈㄨ	功夫	kung fu; martial arts		L1
gōng píng	ㄍㄨㄥ ㄆㄧㄥˊ	公平*	fair		L8
gōng sī	ㄍㄨㄥ ㄙ	公司	company		L7
gōng zhèng	ㄍㄨㄥ ㄓㄥˋ	公正*	fair and just		L5
guó jiā dài biǎo	ㄍㄨㄛˊ ㄐㄧㄚ ㄉㄞˋ ㄅㄧㄠˇ	國家代表*	national representative	国家代表	L8
guó jiā gōng yuán	ㄍㄨㄛˊ ㄐㄧㄚ ㄍㄨㄥ ㄩㄢˊ	國家公園	National Park	国家公园	L1
guó qí	ㄍㄨㄛˊ ㄑㄧˊ	國旗*	country flag	国旗	L10
guó wáng	ㄍㄨㄛˊ ㄨㄤˊ	國王	king	国王	L10

H

hǎi bào	ㄏㄞˇ ㄅㄠˋ	海報	poster	海报	L5
hǎi biān	ㄏㄞˇ ㄅㄧㄢ	海邊	seaside	海边	L1
hǎi fēng	ㄏㄞˇ ㄈㄥ	海風*	sea breeze	海风	L1
hǎi jǐng	ㄏㄞˇ ㄐㄧㄥˇ	海景*	sea view		L1
hǎi yáng	ㄏㄞˇ ㄧㄤˊ	海洋	ocean		L3
hǎo mèng	ㄏㄠˇ ㄇㄥˋ	好夢	sweet dream	好梦	L2
hé	ㄏㄜˊ	河	river		L10
hé liú	ㄏㄜˊ ㄌㄧㄡˊ	河流*	rivers	河流	L10
hòu xuǎn rén	ㄏㄡˋ ㄒㄩㄢˇ ㄖㄣˊ	候選人	candidate	候选人	L5
hú pàn	ㄏㄨˊ ㄆㄢˋ	湖畔*	lakeside	湖畔	L4
hù wài	ㄏㄨˋ ㄨㄞˋ	戶外*	outdoors	户外	L3
hù xiāng	ㄏㄨˋ ㄒㄧㄤ	互相	mutally		L4
hù zhào	ㄏㄨˋ ㄓㄠˋ	護照*	passport	护照	L6
huā	ㄏㄨㄚ	花	spend	花	L6
huā fèi	ㄏㄨㄚ ㄈㄟˋ	花費	expense; expenditure	花费	L7
huá	ㄏㄨㄚˊ	划	row		L10
huá chuán	ㄏㄨㄚˊ ㄔㄨㄢˊ	划船	row a boat	划船	L10
huà	ㄏㄨㄚˋ	畫	draw	画	L5
huà lóng diǎn jīng	ㄏㄨㄚˋ ㄌㄨㄥˊ ㄉㄧㄢˇ ㄐㄧㄥ	畫龍點睛*	add a finishing touch	画龙点睛	L10
huà xué	ㄏㄨㄚˋ ㄒㄩㄝˊ	化學*	chemistry	化学	L2

huī jīn rú tǔ	ㄏㄨㄟ ㄐㄧㄣ ㄖㄨˊ ㄊㄨˇ	揮金如土*	squander; spend money without restraint	挥金如土	L7
huì huà	ㄏㄨㄟˋ ㄏㄨㄚˋ	會話	conversation	会话	L6
huì lù	ㄏㄨㄟˋ ㄌㄨˋ	賄賂*	bribe	贿赂	L5
huì zhǎng	ㄏㄨㄟˋ ㄓㄤˇ	會長	president	会长	L5

J

jī piào	ㄐㄧ ㄆㄧㄠˋ	機票*	air ticket	机票	L6
jī wèi	ㄐㄧ ㄨㄟˋ	機位*	flight seat	机位	L6
jí shǐ	ㄐㄧˊ ㄕˇ	即使	even if		L2
jì jūn	ㄐㄧˋ ㄐㄩㄣ	季軍*	second runner-up	季军	L8
jì niàn bēi	ㄐㄧˋ ㄋㄧㄢˋ ㄅㄟ	紀念碑*	monument	纪念碑	L3
jì niàn guǎn	ㄐㄧˋ ㄋㄧㄢˋ ㄍㄨㄢˇ	紀念館*	memorial hall	纪念馆	L3
jì niàn pǐn	ㄐㄧˋ ㄋㄧㄢˋ ㄆㄧㄣˇ	紀念品	souvenir	纪念品	L1*/L3
jì niàn rì	ㄐㄧˋ ㄋㄧㄢˋ ㄖˋ	紀念日*	anniversary	纪念日	L3
jì xìng	ㄐㄧˋ ㄒㄧㄥˋ	記性	memory	记性	L2
jì xù	ㄐㄧˋ ㄒㄩˋ	繼續	continue	继续	L7
jiā yóu	ㄐㄧㄚ ㄧㄡ	加油	cheer someone on		L8
jià zhào	ㄐㄧㄚˋ ㄓㄠˋ	駕照*	driver's license	驾照	L6
jiān jiào	ㄐㄧㄢ ㄐㄧㄠˋ	尖叫	scream; shriek		L8
jiān zhí	ㄐㄧㄢ ㄓˊ	兼職*	part-time work	兼职	L7
jiǎn dān	ㄐㄧㄢˇ ㄉㄢ	簡單	simple	简单	L5
jiǎn shǎo	ㄐㄧㄢˇ ㄕㄠˇ	減少	reduce; cut down	减少	L7
jiǎng bēi	ㄐㄧㄤˇ ㄅㄟ	獎盃*	trophy	奖杯	L8
jiǎng kè	ㄐㄧㄤˇ ㄎㄜˋ	講課	conduct lessons	讲课	L3
jiǎng pái	ㄐㄧㄤˇ ㄆㄞˊ	獎牌*	medal	奖牌	L8
jiāo ào	ㄐㄧㄠ ㄠˋ	驕傲*	proud	骄傲	L8
jiāo yóu	ㄐㄧㄠ ㄧㄡ	郊遊*	excursion	郊游	L3
jiào táng	ㄐㄧㄠˋ ㄊㄤˊ	教堂*	church		L1
jiē	ㄐㄧㄝ	接	receive (something)		L8
jiē jìn	ㄐㄧㄝ ㄐㄧㄣˋ	接近*	close		L4
jiē lì sài	ㄐㄧㄝ ㄌㄧˋ ㄙㄞˋ	接力賽	relay race	接力赛	L8
jié	ㄐㄧㄝˊ	節	lesson period	节	L9

jié guǒ	ㄐㄧㄝˊ ㄍㄨㄛˇ	結果	result; outcome	结果	L2
jié jiǎn	ㄐㄧㄝˊ ㄐㄧㄢˇ	節儉*	thrifty; frugal	节俭	L7
jié shěng	ㄐㄧㄝˊ ㄕㄥˇ	節省*	save; cut down on	节省	L7
jìn xíng	ㄐㄧㄣˋ ㄒㄧㄥˊ	進行	carry out	进行	L5
jǐng diǎn	ㄐㄧㄥˇ ㄉㄧㄢˇ	景點*	tourist attraction	景点	L1
jìng xuǎn	ㄐㄧㄥˋ ㄒㄩㄢˇ	競選	contest an election	竞选	L5
jū shù	ㄐㄩ ㄕㄨˋ	拘束*	feel restricted		L4
jǔ bàn	ㄐㄩˇ ㄅㄢˋ	舉辦	hold (an event)	举办	L1
jūn zǐ	ㄐㄩㄣ ㄗˇ	君子*	gentleman		L9
jiù shēng yī	ㄐㄧㄡˋ ㄕㄥ ㄧ	救生衣	life jacket		L3

K

kān	ㄎㄢ	看	guard; keep an eye on		L8
kàn fǎ	ㄎㄢˋ ㄈㄚˇ	看法	view; opinion		L2
kāi chú	ㄎㄞ ㄔㄨˊ	開除*	sack; dismiss	开除	L7
kāi huì	ㄎㄞ ㄏㄨㄟˋ	開會	have a meeting	开会	L6
kāi yuán jié liú	ㄎㄞ ㄩㄢˊ ㄐㄧㄝˊ ㄌㄧㄡˊ	開源節流*	increase income and reduce expenditure	开源节流	L7
kē mù	ㄎㄜ ㄇㄨˋ	科目*	subject		L2
kè qín kè jiǎn	ㄎㄜˋ ㄑㄧㄣˊ ㄎㄜˋ ㄐㄧㄢˇ	克勤克儉*	be diligent and frugal	克勤克俭	L7
kǒng zǐ	ㄎㄨㄥˇ ㄗˇ	孔子	Confucius		L9
kǒu shì	ㄎㄡˇ ㄕˋ	口試*	oral examination	口试	L2
kǒu wèi	ㄎㄡˇ ㄨㄟˋ	口味	flavor		L10

L

lán qiú	ㄌㄢˊ ㄑㄧㄡˊ	籃球	basketball	篮球	L8
lǎo rén	ㄌㄠˇ ㄖㄣˊ	老人	elderly		L4
làng fèi	ㄌㄤˋ ㄈㄟˋ	浪費*	waste	浪费	L7
lěng qīng	ㄌㄥˇ ㄑㄧㄥ	冷清	cold and cheerless		L5
lǐ / lǐ jié	ㄌㄧˇ / ㄌㄧˇ ㄐㄧㄝˊ	禮/禮節	code of behavior; protocol	礼/礼节	L9
lǐ yí	ㄌㄧˇ ㄧˊ	禮儀*	etiquette	礼仪*	L9
lì yì	ㄌㄧˋ ㄧˋ	利益*	interest; benefit		L5
lián luò	ㄌㄧㄢˊ ㄌㄨㄛˋ	聯絡	contact	联络	L6
liè	ㄌㄧㄝˋ	列	list		L6
líng yòng qián	ㄌㄧㄥˊ ㄩㄥˋ ㄑㄧㄢˊ	零用錢	pocket money	零用钱	L1

150 Vocabulary Index

lìng wài	ㄌㄧㄥˋ ㄨㄞˋ	另外	in addition		L6
lóng chuán	ㄌㄨㄥˊ ㄔㄨㄢˊ	龍船	dragon boat	龙船	L10
lóng zhōu sài	ㄌㄨㄥˊ ㄓㄡ ㄙㄞˋ	龍舟賽	dragon boat competition	龙舟赛	L10
lǚ guǎn	ㄌㄩˇ ㄍㄨㄢˇ	旅館*	hotel	旅馆	L6
lǚ xíng xiāng	ㄌㄩˇ ㄒㄧㄥˊ ㄒㄧㄤ	旅行箱	travel suitcase		L6
luò xuǎn	ㄌㄨㄛˋ ㄒㄩㄢˇ	落選*	lose an election	落选	L5

M

má fán	ㄇㄚˊ ㄈㄢˊ	麻煩	troublesome; be a bother	麻烦	L3
màn pǎo	ㄇㄢˋ ㄆㄠˇ	慢跑*	jog		L1
měi shí	ㄇㄟˇ ㄕˊ	美食	delicacies		L1
měi shù guǎn	ㄇㄟˇ ㄕㄨˋ ㄍㄨㄢˇ	美術館*	art gallery	美术馆	L1
miǎo	ㄇㄧㄠˇ	秒	seconds		L8
míng cì	ㄇㄧㄥˊ ㄘˋ	名次*	ranking		L8
míng chǎn	ㄇㄧㄥˊ ㄔㄢˇ	名產*	local specialty	名产	L1
míng xìn piàn	ㄇㄧㄥˊ ㄒㄧㄣˋ ㄆㄧㄢˋ	明信片*	postcard		L1
mò shēng	ㄇㄛˋ ㄕㄥ	陌生*	strange; unfamiliar		L4

N

nán guài	ㄋㄢˊ ㄍㄨㄞˋ	難怪	no wonder	难怪	L2
néng lì	ㄋㄥˊ ㄌㄧˋ	能力	capabilities		L5
nián dài	ㄋㄧㄢˊ ㄉㄞˋ	年代	era		L2
nián jì	ㄋㄧㄢˊ ㄐㄧˋ	年紀	age	年纪	L4
nián xīn	ㄋㄧㄢˊ ㄒㄧㄣ	年薪*	annual income	年薪	L7
nóng cūn	ㄋㄨㄥˊ ㄘㄨㄣ	農村*	farm	农村	L4
nòng dǒng	ㄋㄨㄥˋ ㄉㄨㄥˇ	弄懂	having understood	弄懂	L2

P

pá shān	ㄆㄚˊ ㄕㄢ	爬山	mountain climbing		L4
péi bàn	ㄆㄟˊ ㄅㄢˋ	陪伴*	accompany		L4
pèi hé	ㄆㄟˋ ㄏㄜˊ	配合	coordinate		L8
piān sī	ㄆㄧㄢ ㄙ	偏私*	partial; unfair		L5
píng cháng	ㄆㄧㄥˊ ㄔㄤˊ	平常	usual		L4
pò jì lù	ㄆㄛˋ ㄐㄧˋ ㄌㄨˋ	破紀錄*	record-breaking	破纪录	L8

Q

qī dài	ㄑㄧˊ ㄉㄞˋ	期待*	look forward; yearn	期待	L3
qí mǎ	ㄑㄧˊ ㄇㄚˇ	騎馬*	horse riding	骑马	L9
qí zi	ㄑㄧˊ ˙ㄗ	旗子	flag		L10
qì něi	ㄑㄧˋ ㄋㄟˇ	氣餒*	feel discouraged	气馁	L8
qiān wàn	ㄑㄧㄢ ㄨㄢˋ	千萬	be sure to	千万	L3
qiān zhèng	ㄑㄧㄢ ㄓㄥˋ	簽證*	visa	签证	L6
qián shuǐ	ㄑㄧㄢˊ ㄕㄨㄟˇ	潛水*	diving	潜水	L10
qíng xíng	ㄑㄧㄥˊ ㄒㄧㄥˊ	情形	circumstance; situation		L7
qiú yuán	ㄑㄧㄡˊ ㄩㄢˊ	球員	ballgame player	球员	L8

R

rè nào	ㄖㄜˋ ㄋㄠˋ	熱鬧	crowded and lively	热闹	L5
rén ài	ㄖㄣˊ ㄞˋ	仁愛	benevolence and kindness	仁爱	L9
rén mín	ㄖㄣˊ ㄇㄧㄣˊ	人民	people		L10
rén yuán	ㄖㄣˊ ㄩㄢˊ	人員	staff; personnel	人员	L7
rěn bú zhù	ㄖㄣˇ ㄅㄨˊ ㄓㄨˋ	忍不住*	unable to bear; cannot help (doing sth.)		L4
rěn nài	ㄖㄣˇ ㄋㄞˋ	忍耐*	tolerate; endure		L4
rěn ràng	ㄖㄣˇ ㄖㄤˋ	忍讓*	forbear	忍让	L4
rěn shòu	ㄖㄣˇ ㄕㄡˋ	忍受	tolerate		L4
rěn xīn	ㄖㄣˇ ㄒㄧㄣ	忍心*	be hardhearted enough to		L4
rèn wéi	ㄖㄣˋ ㄨㄟˊ	認為	think	认为	L9
ròu	ㄖㄡˋ	肉	meat		L10

S

sēn lín	ㄙㄣ ㄌㄧㄣˊ	森林*	forest		L4
shāng chǎng	ㄕㄤ ㄔㄤˇ	商場	shopping mall	商场	L1
shè jiàn	ㄕㄜˋ ㄐㄧㄢˋ	射箭*	archery		L9
shī / shī shī de	ㄕ / ㄕ ㄕ ˙ㄉㄜ	濕/濕濕的	wet	湿/湿湿的	L3
shī rén	ㄕ ㄖㄣˊ	詩人	poet	诗人	L10
shī wàng	ㄕ ㄨㄤˋ	失望*	to feel disappointed	失望	L3
shī yè	ㄕ ㄧㄝˋ	失業	out of work	失业	L7
shī yè jīn	ㄕ ㄧㄝˋ ㄐㄧㄣ	失業金	unemployment compensation	失业金	L7
shí wù	ㄕˊ ㄨˋ	食物	food		L1
shí xīn	ㄕˊ ㄒㄧㄣ	時薪*	hourly pay	时薪	L7

Vocabulary Index

shí yàn	ㄕˊ ㄧㄢˋ	實驗*	experiment	实验	L2
shì jiàn	ㄕˋ ㄐㄧㄢˋ	事件	event; incident		L2
shì zhǎng	ㄕˋ ㄓㄤˇ	市長	mayor	市长	L10
shài shāng	ㄕㄞˋ ㄕㄤ	晒傷	sunburnt	晒伤	L3
shàng tái	ㄕㄤˋ ㄊㄞˊ	上台	go on stage		L5
shàng wǎng	ㄕㄤˋ ㄨㄤˇ	上網	go on the Internet	上网	L6
shē chǐ	ㄕㄜ ㄔˇ	奢侈*	extravagant		L7
shēng wù	ㄕㄥ ㄨˋ	生物*	biology		L2
shēng wù	ㄕㄥ ㄨˋ	生物	organism		L3
shōu rù	ㄕㄡ ㄖㄨˋ	收入*	income		L7
shú xī	ㄕㄨˊ ㄒㄧ	熟悉	familiar		L4
shuǐ shàng yùn dòng	ㄕㄨㄟˇ ㄕㄤˋ ㄩㄣˋ ㄉㄨㄥˋ	水上運動	water sport	水上运动	L10
shuì guò tóu	ㄕㄨㄟˋ ㄍㄨㄛˋ ㄊㄡˊ	睡過頭*	oversleep	睡过头	L2

T

tài yáng yǎn jìng	ㄊㄞˋ ㄧㄤˊ ㄧㄢˇ ㄐㄧㄥˋ	太陽眼鏡*	sunglasses	太阳眼镜	L3
táng guǒ	ㄊㄤˊ ㄍㄨㄛˇ	糖果	candy		L3
tí qián	ㄊㄧˊ ㄑㄧㄢˊ	提前*	in advance		L6
tǐ cāo	ㄊㄧˇ ㄘㄠ	體操	gymnastics	体操	L8
tiào qí	ㄊㄧㄠˋ ㄑㄧˊ	跳棋*	Chinese checkers		L9
tiào shuǐ	ㄊㄧㄠˋ ㄕㄨㄟˇ	跳水	diving		L8
tóng xiàng	ㄊㄨㄥˊ ㄒㄧㄤˋ	銅像	bronze statue	铜像	L9
tóu / tóu lán	ㄊㄡˊ / ㄊㄡˊ ㄌㄢˊ	投/投籃	shoot a ball through the basket	投/投篮	L8
tóu / tóu piào	ㄊㄡˊ / ㄊㄡˊ ㄆㄧㄠˋ	投/投票	vote		L5
tú àn	ㄊㄨˊ ㄢˋ	圖案*	graphics; pattern	图案	L5
tú huà	ㄊㄨˊ ㄏㄨㄚˋ	圖畫*	drawing	图画	L5
tuán duì	ㄊㄨㄢˊ ㄉㄨㄟˋ	團隊	team	团队	L8
tuì bù	ㄊㄨㄟˋ ㄅㄨˋ	退步	fall behind		L2
tuì xiū	ㄊㄨㄟˋ ㄒㄧㄡ	退休	retire		L4
tuì xiū jīn	ㄊㄨㄟˋ ㄒㄧㄡ ㄐㄧㄣ	退休金*	pension		L4

Vocabulary Index

W

wài bì	ㄨㄞˋ ㄅㄧˋ	外幣*	foreign currency	外币	L6
wài yǔ	ㄨㄞˋ ㄩˇ	外語*	foreign language	外语	L2
wǎn ān	ㄨㄢˇ ㄢ	晚安	good night		L2
wéi qí	ㄨㄟˊ ㄑㄧˊ	圍棋*	Go chess	围棋*	L9
wěi dà	ㄨㄟˇ ㄉㄚˋ	偉大	great; mighty	伟大	L9
wěi rén	ㄨㄟˇ ㄖㄣˊ	偉人	a great man	伟人	L9
wén chóng	ㄨㄣˊ ㄔㄨㄥˊ	蚊蟲*	mosquitoes and insects	蚊虫	L3
wǔ dào	ㄨˇ ㄉㄠˋ	舞蹈*	dance		L1
wù diǎn	ㄨˋ ㄉㄧㄢˇ	誤點*	delay; behind schedule (for transportation)	误点	L6
wù lǐ	ㄨˋ ㄌㄧˇ	物理*	physics		L2

X

xí guàn	ㄒㄧˊ ㄍㄨㄢˋ	習慣	habit; be accustomed to	习惯	L9
xí sú	ㄒㄧˊ ㄙㄨˊ	習俗*	custom	习俗	L10
xì jù	ㄒㄧˋ ㄐㄩˋ	戲劇*	theatrical plays	戏剧	L1
xì xīn	ㄒㄧˋ ㄒㄧㄣ	細心*	meticulous	细心	L2
xià qí	ㄒㄧㄚˋ ㄑㄧˊ	下棋	play chess		L9
xián	ㄒㄧㄢˊ	鹹	savory	咸	L10
xiāng bāo	ㄒㄧㄤ ㄅㄠ	香包*	scent pouch		L10
xiāng xìn	ㄒㄧㄤ ㄒㄧㄣˋ	相信	believe		L5
xiāng xià	ㄒㄧㄤ ㄒㄧㄚˋ	鄉下	countryside	乡下	L1
xiǎng fǎ	ㄒㄧㄤˇ ㄈㄚˇ	想法	thought; opinion		L2
xiǎng shòu	ㄒㄧㄤˇ ㄕㄡˋ	享受	enjoy		L1
xiàng qí	ㄒㄧㄤˋ ㄑㄧˊ	象棋*	Chinese chess		L9
xiǎo rén	ㄒㄧㄠˇ ㄖㄣˊ	小人*	an evil person		L9
xiào wài jiào xué	ㄒㄧㄠˋ ㄨㄞˋ ㄐㄧㄠˋ ㄒㄩㄝˊ	校外教學	field trip	校外教学	L3
xié zhù	ㄒㄧㄝˊ ㄓㄨˋ	協助*	assist	协助	L5
xīn sī	ㄒㄧㄣ ㄙ	心思	thought; efforts		L5
xīn shǎng	ㄒㄧㄣ ㄕㄤˇ	欣賞	appreciate	欣赏	L1
xīn shuǐ	ㄒㄧㄣ ㄕㄨㄟˇ	薪水*	salary; wage	薪水	L7
xīng fèn	ㄒㄧㄥ ㄈㄣˋ	興奮	excited	兴奋	L3
xíng chéng	ㄒㄧㄥˊ ㄔㄥˊ	行程*	itinerary		L6
xíng lǐ	ㄒㄧㄥˊ ㄌㄧˇ	行李*	luggage		L6

xíng lǐ	ㄒㄧㄥˊ ㄌㄧˇ	行禮	salute; pay respect	行礼	L9
xióng wěi	ㄒㄩㄥˊ ㄨㄟˇ	雄偉*	magnificent	雄伟*	L9
xiū xián yú lè	ㄒㄧㄡ ㄒㄧㄢˊ ㄩˊ ㄌㄜˋ	休閒娛樂*	leisure and recreation	休闲娱乐	L1
xǔ xǔ rú shēng	ㄒㄩˇ ㄒㄩˇ ㄖㄨˊ ㄕㄥ	栩栩如生*	life-like		L10
xuǎn jǔ	ㄒㄩㄢˇ ㄐㄩˇ	選舉	election	选举	L5
xuǎn shǒu	ㄒㄩㄢˇ ㄕㄡˇ	選手	athlete; contestant	选手	L8
xué fèi	ㄒㄩㄝˊ ㄈㄟˋ	學費*	school fees	学费	L7
xué shēng huì	ㄒㄩㄝˊ ㄕㄥ ㄏㄨㄟˋ	學生會	student council	学生会	L5

Y

yà jūn	ㄧㄚˋ ㄐㄩㄣ	亞軍*	runner-up	亚军	L8
yán hòu	ㄧㄢˊ ㄏㄡˋ	延後*	postpone	延后	L6
yǎn	ㄧㄢˇ	演	act		L5
yǎn jiǎng	ㄧㄢˇ ㄐㄧㄤˇ	演講	give a speech	演讲	L5
yǎng lǎo yuàn	ㄧㄤˇ ㄌㄠˇ ㄩㄢˋ	養老院*	nursing home; old folks' home	养老院	L4
yě cān	ㄧㄝˇ ㄘㄢ	野餐*	picnic		L3
yī lài	ㄧ ㄌㄞˋ	依賴*	rely on	依赖	L4
yì shù	ㄧˋ ㄕㄨˋ	藝術*	arts	艺术	L1
yīn cǐ	ㄧㄣ ㄘˇ	因此	therefore; hence		L8
yīn yuè huì	ㄧㄣ ㄩㄝˋ ㄏㄨㄟˋ	音樂會	musical concert	音乐会	L1
yìn	ㄧㄣˋ	印	print		L6
yǐng piàn	ㄧㄥˇ ㄆㄧㄢˋ	影片	film		L10
yóu yǒng	ㄧㄡˊ ㄩㄥˇ	游泳	swimming		L1
yú fū	ㄩˊ ㄈㄨ	漁夫	fisherman	渔夫	L3
yǔ xié	ㄩˇ ㄒㄧㄝˊ	雨鞋*	rain boots		L3
yǔ yī	ㄩˇ ㄧ	雨衣	raincoat		L3
yù dìng	ㄩˋ ㄉㄧㄥˋ	預訂*	reserve	预订	L6
yuè tuán	ㄩㄝˋ ㄊㄨㄢˊ	樂團*	orchestra	乐团	L1
yuè xīn	ㄩㄝˋ ㄒㄧㄣ	月薪*	monthly pay	月薪	L7
yuán yīn	ㄩㄢˊ ㄧㄣ	原因	reason		L2
yuǎn lí	ㄩㄢˇ ㄌㄧˊ	遠離*	far apart	远离	L4
yùn dòng jīng shén	ㄩㄣˋ ㄉㄨㄥˋ ㄐㄧㄥ ㄕㄣˊ	運動精神	sportsmanship	运动精神	L8

Vocabulary Index 155

Z

zēng jiā	ㄗㄥ ㄐㄧㄚ	增加*	increase		L7
zhǎn lǎn guǎn	ㄓㄢˇ ㄌㄢˇ ㄍㄨㄢˇ	展覽館*	exhibition center	展览馆	L1
zhèng fǔ	ㄓㄥˋ ㄈㄨˇ	政府	government		L7
zhèng jiàn	ㄓㄥˋ ㄐㄧㄢˋ	政見*	political view	政见	L5
zhèng zhí	ㄓㄥˋ ㄓˊ	正職*	full-time job	正职	L7
zhuàn jì	ㄓㄨㄢˋ ㄐㄧˋ	傳記	biography	传记	L2
zhī chí	ㄓ ㄔˊ	支持*	support	支持	L5
zhī chū	ㄓ ㄔㄨ	支出*	expenditure		L7
zhī shì	ㄓ ㄕˋ	知識	knowledge	知识	L6
zhí yè	ㄓˊ ㄧㄝˋ	職業*	career; job	职业	L7
zhì shèng xiān shī	ㄓˋ ㄕㄥˋ ㄒㄧㄢ ㄕ	至聖先師*	the Great sage and Teacher, a term for Confucius	至圣先师*	L9
zhòng shì	ㄓㄨㄥˋ ㄕˋ	重視*	value; regard highly	重视*	L9
zhù sù	ㄓㄨˋ ㄙㄨˋ	住宿*	accommodation		L6
zhù xuǎn yuán	ㄓㄨˋ ㄒㄩㄢˇ ㄩㄢˊ	助選員*	election agent	助选员	L5
zhǔn bèi	ㄓㄨㄣˇ ㄅㄟˋ	準備	prepare	准备	L2
zhǔn shí	ㄓㄨㄣˇ ㄕˊ	準時*	on time	准时	L6
zī liào	ㄗ ㄌㄧㄠˋ	資料*	information	资料	L6
zì rán kē xué	ㄗˋ ㄖㄢˊ ㄎㄜ ㄒㄩㄝˊ	自然科學*	natural science	自然科学	L2
zì yóu	ㄗˋ ㄧㄡˊ	自由*	free		L4
zòng zi	ㄗㄨㄥˋ ˙ㄗ	粽子	Chinese glutinous rice dumpling		L10
zūn jìng	ㄗㄨㄣ ㄐㄧㄥˋ	尊敬	honor; respect	尊敬	L9
zūn shī zhòng dào	ㄗㄨㄣ ㄕ ㄓㄨㄥˋ ㄉㄠˋ	尊師重道*	respect the teacher and heed his teachings	尊师重道*	L9
zūn zhòng	ㄗㄨㄣ ㄓㄨㄥˋ	尊重*	respect		L9

Name: _____ Class: _____ Date: _____

Lesson 1 **Work It Out**

Survey: Which is a better city to live in?

		Reasons for liking this city	Reasons for disliking this city
City 1: _____	Myself:	1. _____ 2. _____	1. _____ 2. _____
	Others:	_____ _____	_____ _____
City 2: _____	Myself:	1. _____ 2. _____	1. _____ 2. _____
	Others:	_____ _____	_____ _____
City 3: _____	Myself:	1. _____ 2. _____	1. _____ 2. _____
	Others:	_____ _____	_____ _____

City I like most: _____   City I like least: _____

Name: _____ Class: _____ Date: _____

Lesson 2 **Work It Out**

Survey: Preparing for Your Favorite Subject and Activity

Favorite Subjects & Activities

My favorite subject is: _____   My favorite activity is: _____

How I prepare myself: _____   How I prepare myself: _____

_____   _____

_____   _____

_____   _____

_____   _____

Preparation methods of other classmates that I wish to try out:

_____

_____

_____

_____

Learning Styles

Visual:
Total number of students: _____

Auditory:
Total number of students: _____

Tactile:
Total number of students: _____

Kinesthetic:
Total number of students: _____

The most popular learning style in my class: _____

Name: _____ Class: _____ Date: _____

Lesson 6 **Work It Out**

Task: Organizing a Holiday Trip

Our holiday destination: _____

Dice Number	Number of days	Budget per day	Transportation	Souvenirs / for whom?	Others
⚀	10	$100			
⚁	20	$50			
⚂	5	$20			
⚃	14	$150			
⚄	7	$80			
⚅	30	$250			

Go700 Textbook — Lesson 6 Holiday Planning Form

Itinerary:

Hi